San Diego Padres 2021

A Baseball Companion

Edited by Steven Goldman and Bret Sayre

Baseball Prospectus

Craig Brown, Associate Editor
Robert Au, Harry Pavlidis and Amy Pircher, Statistics Editors

Library of Congress Cataloging-in-Publication Data:
paperback
ISBN-13: 978-1-950716-69-2

Project Credits
Cover Design: Ginny Searle
Interior Design and Production: Amy Pircher, Robert Au
Layout: Amy Pircher, Robert Au

Baseball icon courtesy of Uberux, from https://www.shareicon.net/author/uberux

Ballpark diagram courtesy of Lou Spirito/THIRTY81 Project, https://thirty81project.com/

Manufactured in the United States of America
10 9 8 7 6 5 4 3 2 1

Table of Contents

Statistical Introduction

Sports are, fundamentally, a blend of athletic endeavor and storytelling. Baseball, like any other sport, tells its stories in so many ways: in the arc of a game from the stands or a season from the box scores, in photos, or even in numbers. At Baseball Prospectus, we understand that statistics don't replace observation or any of baseball's stories, but complement everything else that makes the game so much fun.

What stats help us with is with patterns and precision, variance and value. This book can help you learn things you may not see from watching a game or hundred, whether it's the path of a career over time or the breadth of the entire MLB. We'd also never ask you to choose between our numbers and the experience of viewing a game from the cheap seats or the comfort of your home; our publication combines running the numbers with observations and wisdom from some of the brightest minds we can find. But if you *do* want to learn more about the numbers beyond what's on the backs of player jerseys, let us help explain.

Offense

We've revised our methodology for determining batting value. Long-time readers of the book will notice that we've retired True Average in favor of a new metric: Deserved Runs Created Plus (DRC+). Developed by Jonathan Judge and our stats team, this statistic measures everything a player does at the plate–reaching base, hitting for power, making outs, and moving runners over–and puts it on a scale where 100 equals league-average performance. A DRC+ of 150 is terrific, a DRC+ of 100 is average and a DRC+ of 75 means you better be an excellent defender.

DRC+ also does a better job than any of our previous metrics in taking contextual factors into account. The model adjusts for how the park affects performance, but also for things like the talent of the opposing pitcher, value of different types of batted-ball events, league, temperature and other factors. It's able to describe a player's expected offensive contribution than any other statistic we've found over the years, and also does a better job of predicting future performance as well.

The other aspect of run-scoring is baserunning, which we quantify using Baserunning Runs. BRR not only records the value of stolen bases (or getting caught in the act), but also accounts for all the stuff that doesn't show up on the back of a baseball card: a runner's ability to go first to third on a single, or advance on a fly ball.

Defense

Where offensive value is *relatively* easy to identify and understand, defensive value is ... not. Over the past dozen years, the sabermetric community has focused mostly on stats based on zone data: a real-live human person records the type of batted ball and estimated landing location, and models are created that give expected outs. From there, you can compare fielders' actual outs to those expected ones. Simple, right?

Unfortunately, zone data has two major issues. First, zone data is recorded by commercial data providers who keep the raw data private unless you pay for it. (All the statistics we build in this book and on our website use public data as inputs.) That hurts our ability to test assumptions or duplicate results. Second, over the years it has become apparent that there's quite a bit of "noise" in zone-based fielding analysis. Sometimes the conclusions drawn from zone data don't hold up to scrutiny, and sometimes the different data provided by different providers don't look anything alike, giving wildly different results. Sometimes the hard-working professional stringers or scorers might unknowingly inflict unconscious bias into the mix: for example good fielders will often be credited with more expected outs despite the data, and ballparks with high press boxes tend to score more line drives than ones with a lower press box.

Enter our Fielding Runs Above Average (FRAA). For most positions, FRAA is built from play-by-play data, which allows us to avoid the subjectivity found in many other fielding metrics. The idea is this: count how many fielding plays are made by a given player and compare that to expected plays for an average fielder at their position (based on pitcher ground ball tendencies and batter handedness). Then we adjust for park and base-out situations.

When it comes to catchers, our methodology is a little different thanks to the laundry list of responsibilities they're tasked with beyond just, well, catching and throwing the ball. By now you've probably heard about "framing" or the art of making umpires more likely to call balls outside the strike zone for strikes. To put this into one tidy number, we incorporate pitch tracking data (for the years it exists) and adjust for important factors like pitcher, umpire, batter and home-field advantage using a mixed-model approach. This grants us a number for how many strikes the catcher is personally adding to (or subtracting from) his pitchers' performance ... which we then convert to runs added or lost using linear weights.

Framing is one of the biggest parts of determining catcher value, but we also take into account blocking balls from going past, whether a scorer deems it a passed ball or a wild pitch. We use a similar approach—one that really benefits from the pitch tracking data that tells us what ends up in the dirt and what doesn't. We also include a catcher's ability to prevent stolen bases and how well they field balls in play, and *finally* we come up with our FRAA for catchers.

Pitching

Both pitching and fielding make up the half of baseball that isn't run scoring: run prevention. Separating pitching from fielding is a tough task, and most recent pitching analysis has branched off from Voros McCracken's famous (and controversial) statement, "There is little if any difference among major-league pitchers in their ability to prevent hits on balls hit in the field of play." The research of the analytic community has validated this to some extent, and there are a host of "defense-independent" pitching measures that have been developed to try and extract the effect of the defense behind a hurler from the pitcher's work.

Our solution to this quandary is Deserved Run Average (DRA), our core pitching metric. DRA seeks to evaluate a pitcher's performance, much like earned run average (ERA), the tried-and-true pitching stat you've seen on every baseball broadcast or box score from the past century, but it's very different. To start, DRA takes an event-by-event look at what the pitchers does, and adjusts the value of that event based on different environmental factors like park, batter, catcher, umpire, base-out situation, run differential, inning, defense, home field advantage, pitcher role and temperature. That mixed model gives us a pitcher's expected contribution, similar to what we do for our DRC+ model for hitters and FRAA model for catchers. (Oh, and we also consider the pitcher's effect on basestealing and on balls getting past the catcher.)

DRA is set to the scale of runs allowed per nine innings (RA9) instead of ERA, which makes DRA's scale slightly higher than ERA's. Because of this, for ease of use, we're supplying DRA-, which is much easier for the reader to parse. As with DRC+, DRA- is an "index" stat, meaning instead of using some arbitrary and shifting number to denote what's "good," average is always 100. The reason that it uses a minus rather than a plus is because like ERA, a lower number is better. Therefore a 75 DRA- describes a performance 25 percent better than average, whereas a 150 DRA- means that either a pitcher is getting extremely lucky with their results, or getting ready to try a new pitch.

Since the last time you picked up an edition of this book, we've also made a few minor changes to DRA to make it better. Recent research into "tunneling"—the act of throwing consecutive pitches that appear similar from a batter's point of view until after the swing decision point–data has given us a new contextual factor to account for in DRA: plate distance. This refers to the distance between successive pitches as they approach the plate, and while it has a smaller effect than factors like velocity or whiff rate, it still can help explain pitcher strikeout rate in our model.

Recently Added Descriptive Statistics

Returning to our 2021 edition of the book are a few figures which recently appeared. These numbers may be a little bit more familiar to those of you who have spent some time investigating baseball statistics.

Fastball Percentage

Our fastball percentage (FA%) statistic measures how frequently a pitcher throws a pitch classified as a "fastball," measured as a percentage of overall pitches thrown. We qualify three types of fastballs:

1. The traditional four-seam fastball;
2. The two-seam fastball or sinker;
3. "Hard cutters," which are pitches that have the movement profile of a cut fastball and are used as the pitcher's primary offering or in place of a more traditional fastball.

For example, a pitcher with a FA% of 67 throws any combination of these three pitches about two-thirds of the time.

Whiff Rate

Everybody loves a swing and a miss, and whiff rate (Whiff%) measures how frequently pitchers induce a swinging strike. To calculate Whiff%, we add up all the pitches thrown that ended with a swinging strike, then divide that number by a pitcher's total pitches thrown. Most often, high whiff rates correlate with high strikeout rates (and overall effective pitcher performance).

Called Strike Probability

Called Strike Probability (CSP) is a number that represents the likelihood that all of a pitcher's pitches will be called a strike while controlling for location, pitcher and batter handedness, umpire and count. Here's how it works: on each pitch, our model determines how many times (out of 100) that a similar pitch was called for a strike given those factors mentioned above, and when normalized for each batter's strike zone. Then we average the CSP for all pitches thrown by a pitcher in a season, and that gives us the yearly CSP percentage you see in the stats boxes.

As you might imagine, pitchers with a higher CSP are more likely to work in the zone, where pitchers with a lower CSP are likely locating their pitches outside the normal strike zone, for better or for worse.

Projections

Many of you aren't turning to this book just for a look at what a player has done, but for a look at what a player is going to do: the PECOTA projections. PECOTA, initially developed by Nate Silver (who has moved on to greater fame as a political analyst), consists of three parts:

1. Major-league equivalencies, which use minor-league statistics to project how a player will perform in the major leagues;
2. Baseline forecasts, which use weighted averages and regression to the mean to estimate a player's current true talent level; and
3. Aging curves, which uses the career paths of comparable players to estimate how a player's statistics are likely to change over time.

With all those important things covered, let's take a look at what's in the book this year.

Team Prospectus

Most of this book is composed of team chapters, with one for each of the 30 major-league franchises. On the first page of each chapter, you'll see a box that contains some of the key statistics for each team as well as a very inviting stadium diagram.

We start with the team name, their unadjusted 2020 win-loss record, and their divisional ranking. Beneath that are a host of other team statistics. **Pythag** presents an adjusted 2020 winning percentage, calculated by taking runs scored per game (**RS/G**) and runs allowed per game (**RA/G**) for the team, and running them through a version of Bill James' Pythagorean formula that was refined and improved by David Smyth and Brandon Heipp. (The formula is called "Pythagenpat," which is equally fun to type and to say.)

Next up is **DRC+**, described earlier, to indicate the overall hitting ability of the team either above or below league-average. Run prevention on the pitching side is covered by **DRA** (also mentioned earlier) and another metric: Fielding Independent Pitching (**FIP**), which calculates another ERA-like statistic based on strikeouts, walks, and home runs recorded. Defensive Efficiency Rating (**DER**) tells us the percentage of balls in play turned into outs for the team, and is a quick fielding shorthand that rounds out run prevention.

After that, we have several measures related to roster composition, as opposed to on-field performance. **B-Age** and **P-Age** tell us the average age of a team's batters and pitchers, respectively. **Payroll** is the combined team payroll for all on-field players, and Doug Pappas' Marginal Dollars per Marginal Win (**M$/MW**) tells us how much money a team spent to earn production above replacement level.

Next to each of these stats, we've listed each team's MLB rank in that category from first to 30th. In this, first always indicates a positive outcome and 30th a negative outcome, except in the case of salary—first is highest.

After the franchise statistics, we share a few items about the team's home ballpark. There's the aforementioned diagram of the park's dimensions (including distances to the outfield wall), a graphic showing the height of the wall from the left-field pole to the right-field pole, and a table showing three-year park factors for the stadium. The park factors are displayed as indexes where 100 is average, 110 means that the park inflates the statistic in question by 10 percent, and 90 means that the park deflates the statistic in question by 10 percent.

On the second page of each team chapter, you'll find three graphs. The first is **Payroll History** and helps you see how the team's payroll has compared to the MLB and divisional average payrolls over time. Payroll figures are current as of January 1, 2021; with so many free agents still unsigned as of this writing, the final 2021 figure will likely be significantly different for many teams. (In the meantime, you can always find the most current data at Baseball Prospectus' Cot's Baseball Contracts page.)

The second graph is **Future Commitments** and helps you see the team's future outlays, if any.

The third graph is **Farm System Ranking** and displays how the Baseball Prospectus prospect team has ranked the organization's farm system since 2007.

After the graphs, we have a **Personnel** section that lists many of the important decision-makers and upper-level field and operations staff members for the franchise, as well as any former Baseball Prospectus staff members who are currently part of the organization. (In very rare circumstances, someone might be on both lists!)

Position Players

After all that information and a thoughtful bylined essay covering each team, we present our player comments. These are also bylined, but due to frequent franchise shifts during the offseason, our bylines are more a rough guide than a perfect accounting of who wrote what.

Each player is listed with the major-league team that employed him as of early January 2021. If a player changed teams after that point via free agency, trade, or any other method, you'll be able to find them in the chapter for their previous squad.

As an example, take a look at the player comment for Padres shortstop Fernando Tatis Jr.: the stat block that accompanies his written comment is at the top of this page. First we cover biographical information (age is as of June 30, 2021) before moving onto the stats themselves. Our statistic columns include standard identifying information like **YEAR**, **TEAM**, **LVL** (level of affiliated play) and **AGE** before getting into the numbers. Next, we provide raw, untranslated

Fernando Tatis Jr. SS

Born: 01/02/99   Age: 22   Bats: R   Throws: R
Height: 6'3"   Weight: 217   Origin: International Free Agent, 2015

YEAR	TEAM	LVL	AGE	PA	R	2B	3B	HR	RBI	BB	K	SB	CS	AVG/OBP/SLG
2018	SA	AA	19	394	77	22	4	16	43	33	109	16	5	.286/.355/.507
2019	SD	MLB	20	372	61	13	6	22	53	30	110	16	6	.317/.379/.590
2020	SD	MLB	21	257	50	11	2	17	45	27	61	11	3	.277/.366/.571
2021 FS	SD	MLB	22	600	95	24	4	31	81	50	165	17	8	.263/.331/.499
2021 DC	SD	MLB	22	628	100	25	4	32	85	53	173	19	8	.263/.331/.499

Comparables: Darryl Strawberry, Bo Bichette, Ronald Acuña Jr.

YEAR	TEAM	LVL	AGE	PA	DRC+	BABIP	BRR	FRAA	WARP
2018	SA	AA	19	394	136	.370	3.0	SS(83): -1.9	2.4
2019	SD	MLB	20	372	118	.410	7.1	SS(83): 0.9	3.4
2020	SD	MLB	21	257	126	.306	0.7	SS(57): -5.5	0.9
2021 FS	SD	MLB	22	600	126	.318	1.7	SS -1	3.9
2021 DC	SD	MLB	22	628	126	.318	1.8	SS -1	4.0

numbers like you might find on the back of your dad's baseball cards: **PA** (plate appearances), **R** (runs), **2B** (doubles), **3B** (triples), **HR** (home runs), **RBI** (runs batted in), **BB** (walks), **K** (strikeouts), **SB** (stolen bases) and **CS** (caught stealing).

Following the basic stats is **Whiff%** (whiff rate), which denotes how often, when a batter swings, he fails to make contact with the ball. Another way to think of this number is an inverse of a hitter's contact rate.

Next, we have unadjusted "slash" statistics: **AVG** (batting average), **OBP** (on-base percentage) and **SLG** (slugging percentage). Following the slash line is **DRC+** (Deserved Runs Created Plus), which we described earlier as total offensive expected contribution compared to the league average.

BABIP (batting average on balls in play) tells us how often a ball in play fell for a hit, and can help us identify whether a batter may have been lucky or not ... but note that high BABIPs also tend to follow the great hitters of our time, as well as speedy singles hitters who put the ball on the ground.

The next item is **BRR** (Baserunning Runs), which covers all of a player's baserunning accomplishments including (but not limited to) swiped bags and failed attempts. Next is **FRAA** (Fielding Runs Above Average), which also includes the number of games previously played at each position noted in parentheses. Multi-position players have only their two most frequent positions listed here, but their total FRAA number reflects all positions played.

Our last column here is **WARP** (Wins Above Replacement Player). WARP estimates the total value of a player, which means for hitters it takes into account hitting runs above average (calculated using the DRC+ model), BRR and FRAA. Then, it makes an adjustment for positions played and gives the player a credit for plate appearances based upon the difference between "replacement level"—which is derived from the quality of players added to a team's roster after the start of the season–and the league average.

The final line just below the stats box is **PECOTA** data, which is discussed further in a following section.

Catchers

Catchers are a special breed, and thus they have earned their own separate box which displays some of the defensive metrics that we've built just for them. As an example, let's check out Yasmani Grandal.

YEAR	TEAM	P. COUNT	FRM RUNS	BLK RUNS	THRW RUNS	TOT RUNS
2018	LAD	16816	15.7	0.8	0.1	16.5
2019	MIL	18740	19.4	1.8	-0.1	21.1
2020	CHW	4830	3.7	0.3	-0.2	3.8
2021	CHW	14430	16.7	-0.6	1.0	17.1
2021	CHW	14430	16.7	0.4	1.0	18.0

The **YEAR** and **TEAM** columns match what you'd find in the other stat box. **P. COUNT** indicates the number of pitches thrown while the catcher was behind the plate, including swinging strikes, fouls and balls in play. **FRM RUNS** is the total run value the catcher provided (or cost) his team by influencing the umpire to call strikes where other catchers did not. **BLK RUNS** expresses the total run value above or below average for the catcher's ability to prevent wild pitches and passed balls. **THRW RUNS** is calculated using a similar model as the previous two statistics, and it measures a catcher's ability to throw out basestealers but also to dissuade them from testing his arm in the first place. It takes into account factors like the pitcher (including his delivery and pickoff move) and baserunner (who could be as fast as Billy Hamilton or as slow as Yonder Alonso). **TOT RUNS** is the sum of all of the previous three statistics.

Pitchers

Let's give our pitchers a turn, using 2020 AL Cy Young winner Shane Bieber as our example. Take a look at his stat block: the first line and the **YEAR**, **TEAM**, **LVL** and **AGE** columns are the same as in the position player example earlier.

Here too, we have a series of columns that display raw, unadjusted statistics compiled by the pitcher over the course of a season: **W** (wins), **L** (losses), **SV** (saves), **G** (games pitched), **GS** (games started), **IP** (innings pitched), **H** (hits allowed) and **HR** (home runs allowed). Next we have two statistics that are rates: **BB/9** (walks per nine innings) and **K/9** (strikeouts per nine innings), before returning to the unadjusted K (strikeouts).

Next up is **GB%** (ground ball percentage), which is the percentage of all batted balls that were hit on the ground, including both outs and hits. Remember, this is based on observational data and subject to human error, so please approach this with a healthy dose of skepticism.

BABIP (batting average on balls in play) is calculated using the same methodology as it is for position players, but it often tells us more about a pitcher than it does a hitter. With pitchers, a high BABIP is often due to poor defense or bad luck, and can often be an indicator of potential rebound, and a low BABIP may be cause to expect performance regression. (A typical league-average BABIP is close to .290-.300.)

The metrics **WHIP** (walks plus hits per inning pitched) and **ERA** (earned run average) are old standbys: WHIP measures walks and hits allowed on a per-inning basis, while ERA measures earned runs on a nine-inning basis. Neither of these stats are translated or adjusted.

DRA- (Deserved Run Average) was described at length earlier, and measures how the pitcher "deserved" to perform compared to other pitchers. Please note that since we lack all the data points that would make for a "real" DRA for minor-league events, the DRA- displayed for minor league partial-seasons is based off of different data. (That data is a modified version of our cFIP metric, which you can find more information about on our website.)

Shane Bieber   RHP

Born: 05/31/95   Age: 26   Bats: R   Throws: R
Height: 6'3"   Weight: 200   Origin: Round 4, 2016 Draft (#122 overall)

YEAR	TEAM	LVL	AGE	W	L	SV	G	GS	IP	H	HR	BB/9	K/9	K	GB%	BABIP
2018	AKR	AA	23	3	0	0	5	5	31	26	1	0.3	8.7	30	47.3%	.278
2018	COL	AAA	23	3	1	0	8	8	48²	30	3	1.1	8.7	47	52.0%	.227
2018	CLE	MLB	23	11	5	0	20	19	114²	130	13	1.8	9.3	118	46.2%	.356
2019	CLE	MLB	24	15	8	0	34	33	214¹	186	31	1.7	10.9	259	44.4%	.298
2020	CLE	MLB	25	8	1	0	12	12	77¹	46	7	2.4	14.2	122	48.4%	.267
2021 FS	CLE	MLB	26	10	6	0	26	26	150	121	18	2.1	11.7	195	45.5%	.297
2021 DC	CLE	MLB	26	14	7	0	30	30	196.7	159	24	2.1	11.7	257	45.5%	.297

Comparables: Luis Severino, Danny Salazar, Joe Musgrove

YEAR	TEAM	LVL	AGE	WHIP	ERA	DRA-	WARP	MPH	FB%	WHF	CSP
2018	AKR	AA	23	0.87	1.16	61	0.9				
2018	COL	AAA	23	0.74	1.66	69	1.2				
2018	CLE	MLB	23	1.33	4.55	74	2.6	94.7	57.4%	26.2%	
2019	CLE	MLB	24	1.05	3.28	75	4.9	94.4	45.8%	30.8%	
2020	CLE	MLB	25	0.87	1.63	53	2.6	95.3	53.6%	40.7%	
2021 FS	CLE	MLB	26	1.04	2.44	64	4.4	94.7	50.0%	33.2%	44.2%
2021 DC	CLE	MLB	26	1.04	2.44	64	5.8	94.7	50.0%	33.2%	44.2%

Just like with hitters, **WARP** (Wins Above Replacement Player) is a total value metric that puts pitchers of all stripes on the same scale as position players. We use DRA as the primary input for our calculation of WARP. You might notice that relief pitchers (due to their limited innings) may have a lower WARP than you were expecting or than you might see in other WARP-like metrics. WARP does not take leverage into account, just the actions a pitcher performs and the expected value of those actions … which ends up judging high-leverage relief pitchers differently than you might imagine given their prestige and market value.

MPH gives you the pitcher's 95th percentile velocity for the noted season, in order to give you an idea of what the *peak* fastball velocity a pitcher possesses. Since this comes from our pitch-tracking data, it is not publicly available for minor-league pitchers.

Finally, we display the three new pitching metrics we described earlier. **FB%** (fastball percentage) gives you the percentage of fastballs thrown out of all pitches. **WHF** (whiff rate) tells you the percentage of swinging strikes induced out of all pitches. **CSP** (called strike probability) expresses the likelihood of all pitches thrown to result in a called strike, after controlling for factors like handedness, umpire, pitch type, count and location.

PECOTA

All players have PECOTA projections for 2021, as well as a set of other numbers that describe the performance of comparable players according to PECOTA. All projections for 2021 are for the player at the date we went to press in early January and are projected into the league and park context as indicated by the team abbreviation. (Note that players at very low levels of the minors are too unpredictable to assess using these numbers.) All PECOTA projected statistics represent a player's projected major-league performance.

How we're doing that is a little different this season. There are really two different values that go into the final stat line that you see for PECOTA: How a player performs, and how much playing time he'll be given to perform it. In the past we've estimated playing time based on each team's roster and depth charts, and we'll continue to do that. These projections are denoted as **2021 DC**.

But in many cases, a player won't be projected for major-league playing time; most of the time this is because they aren't projected to be major-league players at all, but still developing as prospects. Or perhaps a player will provide Triple-A depth, only to have an opportunity open up because of injury. For these purposes, we're also supplying a second projection, labeled **2021 FS**, or full season. This is what we would project the player to provide in 600 plate appearances or 150 innings pitched.

Below the projections are the player's three highest-scoring comparable players as determined by PECOTA. All comparables represent a snapshot of how the listed player was performing at the same age as the current player, so if a

23-year-old pitcher is compared to Bartolo Colón, he's actually being compared to a 23-year-old Colón, not the version that pitched for the Rangers in 2018, nor to Colón's career as a whole.

A few points about pitcher projections. First, we aren't yet projecting peak velocity, so that column will be blank in the PECOTA lines. Second, projecting DRA is trickier than evaluating past performance, because it is unclear how deserving each pitcher will be of his anticipated outcomes. However, we know that another DRA-related statistic–contextual FIP or cFIP-estimates future run scoring very well. So for PECOTA, the projected DRA- figures you see are based on the past cFIPs generated by the pitcher and comparable players over time, along with the other factors described above.

If you're familiar with PECOTA, then you'll have noticed that the projection system often appears bullish on players coming off a bad year and bearish on players coming off a good year. (This is because the system weights several previous seasons, not just the most recent one.) In addition, we publish the 50th percentile projections for each player–which is smack in the middle of the range of projected production—which tends to mean PECOTA stat lines don't often have extreme results like 40 home runs or 250 strikeouts in a given season. In essence, PECOTA doesn't project very many extreme seasons.

Managers

After all those wonderful team chapters, we've got statistics for each big-league manager, all of whom are organized by alphabetical order. Here you'll find a block including an extraordinary amount of information collected from each manager's entire career. For more information on the acronyms and what they mean, please visit the Glossary at www.baseballprospectus.com.

There is one important metric that we'd like to call attention to, and you'll find it next to each manager's name: **wRM+** (weighted reliever management plus). Developed by Rob Arthur and Rian Watt, wRM+ investigates how good a manager is at using their best relievers during the moments of highest leverage, using both our proprietary DRA metric as well as Leverage Index. wRM+ is scaled to a league average of 100, and a wRM+ of 105 indicates that relievers were used approximately five percent "better" than average. On the other hand, a wRM+ of 95 would tell us the team used its relievers five percent "worse" than the average team.

While wRM+ does not have an extremely strong correlation with a manager, it is statistically significant; this means that a manager is not *entirely* responsible for a team's wRM+, but does have some effect on that number.

Part 1: Team Analysis

Performance Graphs

Payroll History (in millions)

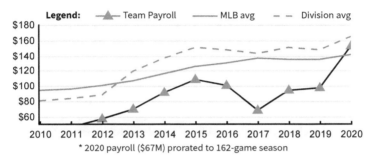

* 2020 payroll ($67M) prorated to 162-game season

Future Commitments (in millions)

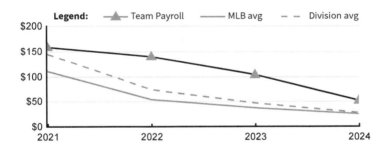

Farm System Ranking

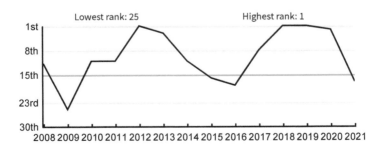

2020 Team Performance

ACTUAL STANDINGS

Team	W	L	Pct
LAD	43	17	0.717
SD	**37**	**23**	**0.617**
SF	29	31	0.483
COL	26	34	0.433
ARI	25	35	0.417

dWIN% STANDINGS

Team	W	L	Pct
LAD	37	23	0.624
SD	**34**	**26**	**0.567**
SF	27	33	0.465
ARI	23	37	0.386
COL	22	38	0.375

TOP HITTERS

Player	WARP
Manny Machado	2.1
Wil Myers	1.8
Fernando Tatis Jr.	0.9

TOP PITCHERS

Player	WARP
Dinelson Lamet	1.8
Zach Davies	0.9
Trevor Rosenthal	0.7

VITAL STATISTICS

Statistic Name	Value	Rank
Pythagenpat	.639	2nd
dWin%	.567	3rd
Runs Scored per Game	5.42	3rd
Runs Allowed per Game	4.02	8th
Deserved Runs Created Plus	110	4th
Deserved Run Average Minus	89	7th
Fielding Independent Pitching	4.01	6th
Defensive Efficiency Rating	.703	14th
Batter Age	27.3	5th
Pitcher Age	28.2	14th
Payroll	$67.0M	10th
Marginal $ per Marginal Win	$2.6M	12th

2021 Team Projections

PROJECTED STANDINGS

Team	W	L	Pct	+/-
LAD	104.4	57.6	0.644	-11
With Dustin May ready and David Price returning, adding Trevor Bauer was purely lapidary. Still, they're almost alone in their willingness to put up or shut up.				
SD	95.4	66.6	0.589	-4
Not just Blake Snell, but Yu Darvish and Joe Musgrove; not just Ha-Seong Kim, but Jurickson Profar, all without trading a starting player.				
ARI	79.2	82.8	0.489	11
Mike Hazen is a good trader, but ownership continues to confine him to corner-store bartering.				
SF	74.9	87.1	0.462	-3
Most of their individual moves were small, but the Giants' winter work amounts to the first step toward pivoting from a rebuild to contending.				
COL	58.9	103.1	0.364	-11
The time was ripe for a rebuild, but the return for Nolan Arenado is not a confidence-inspiring start.				

TOP PROJECTED HITTERS

Player	WARP
Fernando Tatis Jr.	4.0
Manny Machado	3.7
Trent Grisham	2.8

TOP PROJECTED PITCHERS

Player	WARP
Yu Darvish	3.9
Blake Snell	3.6
Chris Paddack	2.9

FARM SYSTEM REPORT

Top Prospect	Number of Top 101 Prospects
CJ Abrams, #10	4

KEY DEDUCTIONS

Player	WARP
Zach Davies	1.8
Kirby Yates	1.2
Garrett Richards	1.1
Joey Lucchesi	1.0
Francisco Mejía	0.7
Jason Castro	0.6
David Bednar	0.3
Luis Patiño	0.3

KEY ADDITIONS

Player	WARP
Yu Darvish	3.9
Blake Snell	3.6
Joe Musgrove	2.5
Victor Caratini	0.4

Team Personnel

Executive Vice President, General Manager
A.J. Preller

Vice President, Assistant General Manager
Fred Uhlman, Jr.

Senior Advisor/Director of Player Personnel
Logan White

Assistant General Manager
Josh Stein

Manager
Jayce Tingler

BP Alumni
David Cameron

Petco Park Stats

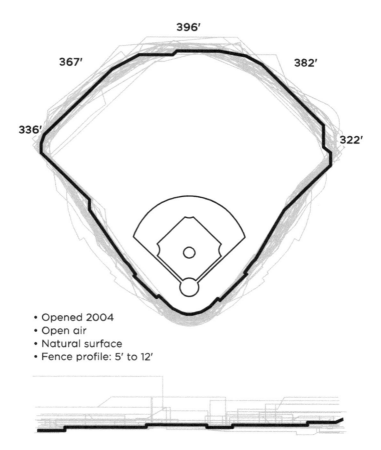

396'

367'

382'

336'

322'

- Opened 2004
- Open air
- Natural surface
- Fence profile: 5' to 12'

Three-Year Park Factors

Runs	Runs/RH	Runs/LH	HR/RH	HR/LH
96	97	94	96	91

Padres Team Analysis

Eric Hosmer has a look on his face. You know the one. Scott Boras is sitting next to him on the dais and, in the course of discussing what the freshly signed first baseman could mean to the San Diego Padres, has launched into a metaphoric foretelling of a volcanic eruption. Hosmer, understandably, appears to be knocked off his mental balance—the way you might be when an uncle makes the pivot from frozen waffles to the impending arrival of Judgment Day.

"I think the organization is a volcano of hot talent lava," Boras says. "To turn that lava into major league rock, that's a hard thing to do. It's a very, very difficult thing to do," the agent continues. "What Eric Hosmer brings is he went through all that in Kansas City. He along with many people were all prospects. They were, too, that major league lava, and they turned into championship rocks. When you can have a young veteran champion, I think your chances of guiding lava into rocks are pretty good, and I think that's the destiny and the plan."

That word: *plan*. The Padres always seem to have plans. One of the most salient lessons of semi-recent psychological research—and extremely recent universal human experience—dictates that we are terrible at predicting the future. The Padres are proof that teams often are, too. Bad at assessing the risks we face and bad at gauging the chances of our dreams coming true. It's a testament to the power of human adaptability that we survive putting ourselves in so many positions to escape.

As baseball fans, we suffer from unrealistic optimism: Our rebuild isn't in danger of stalling out and drifting perilously back toward the launch pad (that only happens to the Phillies). Every prospect will land. Every trade will pay dividends tomorrow. Our core will coalesce into not just a moment of glory, but an era of unmatched prosperity. The modern analytical movement has moved to counter this blindness, throwing open the shutters on baseball's dreamers. But then there are the Padres, who court the peril of grandiose expectations. From an initial abject failure sprung a prophecy brought to a sort of fruition, and from that an even bigger dream that suddenly involves Blake Snell and Yu Darvish, a new spectacular unseen promise.

⚾　　⚾　　⚾

On the day the club inked Hosmer, the gathering heat emanated chiefly from Fernando Tatis Jr., who was already a top-10 prospect in baseball. Lean, lanky and impossibly springy, the shortstop is the self-evident icon of the Padres in a microcosmic way almost too apt to be possible. Tatis is kinetic and potential energy in one. He was brought to the organization in the dismantling of A.J. Preller's first swing at contention—a fruit of the fire—and his rapid ascent from James Shields trade deep cut to San Diego Baseball Frodo heralded that this plan might be the one to rule them all.

These heightened hopes were built on something sturdier, or at least something resembling the game's modern model. Build a system, promote cheap young stars, smooth out the roster through free agency. But as the Los Angeles Dodgers' dominance of the NL West marched on, Hosmer didn't turn out to be the immediate spark San Diego might have hoped. The new plan was beginning to look suspiciously similar to the old plan, the one that brought Matt Kemp's infectious smile and arthritic hip, a brief and costly glimmer of hope. By the time the Boston Red Sox thwarted the Dodgers and defensive savant Yasmani Grandal in the 2018 World Series, the franchises were reaching feverish levels of anxious yearning—the Dodgers for rings, the Padres for relevance.

Needing to feel some shift, or perhaps to provide a boost while they waited, the Padres leapt at the chance to add Manny Machado in free agency. Meanwhile, the farm system blossomed. When Tatis and Machado made their San Diego debuts simultaneously on Opening Day 2019, side by side, it was hard not to think the team had definitely, absolutely entered a new phase.

Seven months and 85 losses later, the Padres fired manager Andy Green. A few days after that, then-chairman Ron Fowler called the decisive late-season slump his "worst 2 ½ months of ownership." In a conversation with players, then a chat with fans, and then in an interview with the San Diego Union-Tribune, he was surprisingly frank (refreshingly so, in the contemporary world of ownership margin-measuring).

"I said if we don't win in 2020, heads will roll," Fowler told the paper.

⚾   ⚾   ⚾

The Padres won.

In the hushed, faraway world of 2020, they were the team that did the most to dissolve the screen between viewer and action. Tatis rocketed out to the best start of any player in the league, drawing the attention of more and more wandering eyes. When he pounced on an innocuous 3-0 pitch against the lowly Texas Rangers, it sparked and absorbed all the oxygen in the baseball ecosystem for days on end. With takes burning around them, the Padres reacted with a delirious run of grand slams that cemented their status as the best circus in town for a socially distanced populace. The Padres, their fanbase perennially hemmed into the corner of the country by Dodger blue, was rapidly becoming every city's second-favorite team.

Machado turned the page on his middling 2019 season so thoroughly that it was eventually he, not Tatis, who figured most prominently in MVP discussions. But it wasn't just the new wave that led this charge; the punchlines of old forgotten plans re-emerged. Hosmer hit like a star as well as a leader. The enigmatic Wil Myers posted a career (third of a) year. Jurickson Profar played well, and often.

The schedule provided no shortage of chances to measure progress. Sequestered to regional play for 2020, the Padres were sentenced to contest one-sixth of their games against the Dodgers. From the first meeting, on Aug. 3, the games were rapid-fire exercises in building and shaking confidence. Trent Grisham homered against Walker Buehler as part of a torrid start. Little-discussed trade acquisition Jake Cronenworth appeared as a replacement for an injured Eric Hosmer and started making leaping grabs at first base. Dinelson Lamet faced off with Dustin May. The Padres lost the series, 2-1, but felt credible.

A week later they again hurled themselves up against that overstuffed behemoth of talent, this time splitting a four-game set. It appeared, as the two teams stampeded toward and into the playoffs, that their only NL rivals were each other. Still, the Padres almost stumbled on the way to their October trial.

And it was in the NL wild-card series against St. Louis that the Padres put the stench of the contenders that weren't behind them. Backed into a corner in the three-game series, the grave, metallic taste of a fluke crept in. What if the late season fade was a sign of things to come for Tatis? What if it was just a hot 60 games? What if they don't do it in a full season? What if they never do this in front of actual corporeal fans?

Mid-2010s despair was burbling to the surface when Tatis and Machado finally struck in the sixth inning of Game 2, erasing a four-run deficit with back-to-back home runs, darts into the seats beyond left field. The coup de grâce arrived an inning later, as Tatis belted a backbreaking second homer and propelled his bat into the sky. The camera trembled in a hollowed out park, an eruption. As they left home for the last time in 2020, after vanquishing their foes in Game 3, fans assembled in person outside the gates of Petco Park. They waited for the players who had lifted their expectations and they cheered them on—reveling in the glow, fanning the flames.

San Diego's breakout season eventually ended at the hands of those Dodgers, the juggernauts they hope to replace. But there were mitigating circumstances behind the Division Series sweep. Injuries rendered ascendant ace Lamet and trade deadline acquisition Mike Clevinger moot, kneecapping the starting rotation and eventually the whole staff. The pitching wore so thin that prospect Ryan Weathers was summoned to make his major-league debut in the least friendly of circumstances. In the end, it gave Padres fans a wide berth to keep chasing the comparison, and Preller an obvious area for upgrades. By the time 2020 actually ended, Padres fans could view their weakness as fortified, their Dodgers problem as addressed. They could say "Wait til next year" not with resignation, but with an edge.

⚾   ⚾   ⚾

"Affective forecasting" is the practice of predicting how you will feel in the future. Daniel Gilbert and Timothy Wilson coined the term in the 1990s, giving a name to the undercurrent that sways so many decisions. While they were at it, they documented just how bad we are at this sort of prediction too.

We overestimate how far the pendulum will swing in either direction, traumatic or triumphant. The good news, as Gilbert explained in an interview with Smithsonian Magazine, is that people tend to recover from tragedy much more quickly and completely than they would ever expect. He continues: "The bad news is that the good things that happen to us don't feel as good or last as long as we think they will. So all that wonderful stuff we're aiming for—winning the lottery, getting promoted, whatever we think will change our lives—probably won't do it after all. We're resilient in both directions. We rebound from distress but we also rebound from joy."

"Wait til next year" is the universal baseball fan signal for this subconscious rebound, and also for a particular sort of unquenchable dissatisfaction. The long-smoldering Los Angeles core no longer needs to utter that rite of the fall. They proceeded to win it all in 2020, finally, ending a drought that lasted 30 years and intensified into a pox upon a mighty team's house over the past half decade. Like if the Cubs or Red Sox sagas were adapted to a one-act play.

Sports are arranged to unravel the hedonic treadmill problem by dropping an actual destination on the map once annually and firing the starting gun. It's an appealingly condensed, low-stakes plaything version of the pursuit of happiness where a discrete goal is either achieved or missed. It's hard to say it works any better than our real life attempts at setting satisfying goals, though.

Relevance and rings. Fans crave one until the moment they have it. Then they crave the other.

If there was a single moment that the city of San Diego crossed that line, it was on December 28, when the organization made its own priorities transparent. In the span of 12 hours the Padres rotation was remade via the thunderous dual trades for Darvish and Snell. While both men are under contract for three years, there can be no confusion: The volcano is ready.

⚾   ⚾   ⚾

There isn't much evidence the two forms of desire can coexist within the same collective psyche. But if there's ever been a team with the conditions to forge a fusion, it might be these Padres.

Birthed in 1969, the franchise has still never won a World Series, but it doesn't need that phrase either. The marketing department has to talk of trophies now, but fans should resist the urge to pin this group's hopes to a title. Yes, championships are the salvation we are promised—and few have ever unleashed more joy into the world than Chicago's triumph in 2016. They're also exactly the sort of carrots that dart beyond one's grasp. When thirst for a ring rules all, the quest to quench it can turn into a depressing rush to nowhere. The day when this team and the memories it created get parted out for Single-A arms will come soon enough.

In the realm of stimuli-seeking fandom, the choice between relief and revelation should be an obvious one. How sad it would be to fixate on the future, after all, when the Padres are so damn fun in the present? But as with rapturous doomsday predictions or, say, volcanic eruptions, calamity and creation are sometimes hard to separate.

The modern game of baseball makes its money in the future tense: the projection, the prospect list, the promises. Blake Snell and Yu Darvish trying on their new jerseys for the first time. Ownership reinforcing their beliefs. *We're going to win.* And yet the moments where we can live most vicariously and most vividly through a baseball team dance on the tightrope between that calamity and creation. Like Hosmer's mad dash home in the clinching game of the 2015 World Series—dynamic, breathtaking and emblematic of those Royals teams—the peak of fan experience is in heated moments of fluidity. It's the swing of a Tatis Jr. home run, existing in all tenses at once.

This team's temperature is still rising. It could be that this Padres core wins a title, or several titles. It could be they win no titles at all. Yes, the prediction Boras made for the Padres was of championships. It envisioned lava turning to rock, a denouement; cooling, solidifying. But the part that spoke to the energy of the moment, that made it on the T-shirt, was the lava.

—Zach Crizer is the baseball editor at Yahoo Sports.

Part 2: Player Analysis

PLAYER COMMENTS WITH GRAPHS

Victor Caratini   C

Born: 08/17/93   Age: 27   Bats: S   Throws: R
Height: 6'1"   Weight: 215   Origin: Round 2, 2013 Draft (#65 overall)

YEAR	TEAM	LVL	AGE	PA	R	2B	3B	HR	RBI	BB	K	SB	CS	AVG/OBP/SLG
2018	IOW	AAA	24	137	13	7	0	4	22	18	25	0	0	.313/.409/.478
2018	CHC	MLB	24	200	21	7	0	2	21	12	42	0	0	.232/.293/.304
2019	CHC	MLB	25	279	31	11	0	11	34	29	59	1	0	.266/.348/.447
2020	CHC	MLB	26	132	10	7	0	1	16	12	31	0	1	.241/.333/.328
2021 FS	SD	MLB	27	600	72	19	1	16	67	56	141	0	1	.234/.316/.368
2021 DC	SD	MLB	27	126	15	4	0	3	14	11	29	0	0	.234/.316/.368

Comparables: Sal Fasano, Chris Snyder, Ben Davis

The advent of the universal DH seemed like a prime opportunity for the Cubs to move Kyle Schwarber out of left field. Instead, they prioritized finding additional playing time for Caratini, who hit like a starter in 2019 but remained blocked by Willson Contreras at catcher. Caratini received more starts at DH than any other Cub,

YEAR	TEAM	P. COUNT	FRM RUNS	BLK RUNS	THRW RUNS	TOT RUNS
2018	CHC	4981	-1.0	0.3	0.1	-0.6
2018	IOW	2846	-1.9	0.0	-0.1	-2.0
2019	CHC	6899	3.4	0.9	-0.1	4.2
2020	CHC	2834	0.9	-0.1	0.0	0.8
2021	SD	3608	0.2	-0.3	0.1	0.0
2021	SD	3608	0.2	0.6	0.1	0.9

but his offensive breakout didn't carry over—he struck out more frequently, walked less and his power evaporated entirely. Once thought to be undercast as a backup, Caratini's step backward qualifies as a disappointment. Oh well; he remains a solid defender who should continue to find work spelling starters behind the dish. He'll try to find room to work in a crowded Padres backstop rotation following a December trade, though his relationship with Yu Darvish should give him a leg up.

YEAR	TEAM	LVL	AGE	PA	DRC+	BABIP	BRR	FRAA	WARP
2018	IOW	AAA	24	137	138	.364	-0.6	C(18): -2.2, 1B(12): 1.6, 3B(1): -0.0	0.8
2018	CHC	MLB	24	200	69	.290	-0.6	C(37): -0.8, 1B(20): 0.5, 3B(3): -0.0	0.0
2019	CHC	MLB	25	279	102	.305	-1.4	C(59): 3.7, 1B(23): -0.5, 3B(2): -0.1	1.5
2020	CHC	MLB	26	132	85	.321	-1.5	C(22): -0.4, 1B(3): 0.0	0.0
2021 FS	SD	MLB	27	600	92	.287	-0.7	C 3, 1B 0	1.7
2021 DC	SD	MLB	27	126	92	.287	-0.2	C 1	0.4

Victor Caratini, continued

Batted Ball Distribution

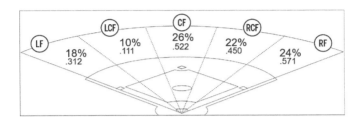

Strike Zone vs LHP   Strike Zone vs RHP

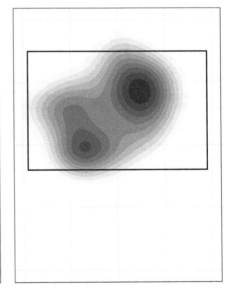

Jake Cronenworth   SS

Born: 01/21/94   Age: 27   Bats: L   Throws: R
Height: 6'0"   Weight: 187   Origin: Round 7, 2015 Draft (#208 overall)

YEAR	TEAM	LVL	AGE	PA	R	2B	3B	HR	RBI	BB	K	SB	CS	AVG/OBP/SLG
2018	MTG	AA	24	470	75	18	4	4	50	43	69	21	3	.254/.323/.344
2018	DUR	AAA	24	26	4	3	0	0	2	1	5	1	0	.240/.269/.360
2019	DUR	AAA	25	406	75	26	4	10	45	49	62	12	5	.334/.429/.520
2020	SD	MLB	26	192	26	15	3	4	20	18	30	3	1	.285/.354/.477
2021 FS	SD	MLB	27	600	70	30	4	12	68	54	122	5	2	.258/.334/.400
2021 DC	SD	MLB	27	526	61	26	4	10	60	47	107	4	2	.258/.334/.400

Comparables: Josh Rutledge, Justin Sellers, Luis Valbuena

The word "cronen" is derived from a Middle Dutch word that means "to crown." That seems fitting, as Cronenworth demonstrated his worth for the NL Rookie of the Year Award. You usually don't see players get traded away from the Rays and get better. Cronenworth proved to be an exception. Though he was excellent in Triple-A in 2019, the Rays seemingly decided they had enough middle-infield depth to include him in the Tommy Pham trade. Given that Cronenworth seemed more likely to be a bench piece (and, perhaps, also a bullpen piece), it was a worthwhile gamble. Credit to the Padres for seeing something more, and credit to Cronenworth for making the most of his shot, but beware the small samples of 2020: Cronenworth cooled down the stretch and we won't know what's signal and what's noise for a while.

YEAR	TEAM	LVL	AGE	PA	DRC+	BABIP	BRR	FRAA	WARP
2018	MTG	AA	24	470	106	.291	5.6	SS(59): -4.6, 3B(28): 5.4, 2B(18): -2.5	1.6
2018	DUR	AAA	24	26	93	.300	1.1	3B(5): -0.5, 2B(1): 0.0, SS(1): -0.2	0.1
2019	DUR	AAA	25	406	137	.382	0.7	SS(64): -1.7, 2B(11): 1.3, P(7): 0.1	3.4
2020	SD	MLB	26	192	115	.324	-0.1	2B(38): -1.1, SS(11): -1.3, 1B(10): 1.2	0.8
2021 FS	SD	MLB	27	600	101	.315	0.0	SS -1, 2B 0	1.7
2021 DC	SD	MLB	27	526	101	.315	0.0	LF 0, SS -1	1.4

Jake Cronenworth, continued

Batted Ball Distribution

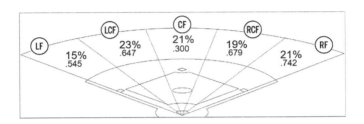

Strike Zone vs LHP   ## Strike Zone vs RHP

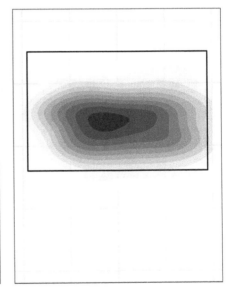

Trent Grisham CF

Born: 11/01/96   Age: 24   Bats: L   Throws: L
Height: 5'11"   Weight: 224   Origin: Round 1, 2015 Draft (#15 overall)

YEAR	TEAM	LVL	AGE	PA	R	2B	3B	HR	RBI	BB	K	SB	CS	AVG/OBP/SLG
2018	BLX	AA	21	405	45	10	2	7	31	63	87	11	3	.233/.356/.337
2019	BLX	AA	22	283	34	14	3	13	41	44	50	6	4	.254/.371/.504
2019	SA	AAA	22	158	37	8	3	13	30	23	22	6	1	.381/.471/.776
2019	MIL	MLB	22	183	24	6	2	6	24	20	47	1	0	.231/.328/.410
2020	SD	MLB	23	252	42	8	3	10	26	31	64	10	1	.251/.352/.456
2021 FS	SD	MLB	24	600	87	23	4	21	65	74	165	8	4	.233/.334/.419
2021 DC	SD	MLB	24	617	90	23	5	21	66	76	170	8	4	.233/.334/.419

Comparables: Rick Monday, Larry Hisle, Mack Jones

Grisham was always a frustrating prospect coming up through the Brewers' system. The former 15th-overall pick never quite lived up to expectations, especially for someone who was considered to be a "safe" hitting prospect. After an underwhelming major-league debut in 2019, the Brewers seemingly gave up on him and traded him to San Diego as part of the Luis Urías deal. Now that looks like a mistake. A notoriously passive hitter, Grisham started swinging at pitches in the zone more frequently while still drawing plenty of walks. Even if his true-talent level is that of a below-average hitter, the fact that he can stick in center field should make him a starter for years to come.

YEAR	TEAM	LVL	AGE	PA	DRC+	BABIP	BRR	FRAA	WARP
2018	BLX	AA	21	405	108	.292	-1.8	RF(85): 3.5, LF(15): 1.1, CF(6): 2.3	1.0
2019	BLX	AA	22	283	161	.269	-0.4	CF(59): 3.3	3.1
2019	SA	AAA	22	158	192	.384	0.3	CF(31): 3.3, LF(3): -0.1	2.6
2019	MIL	MLB	22	183	89	.283	2.2	CF(21): -1.1, LF(17): -1.8, RF(16): 0.3	0.3
2020	SD	MLB	23	252	94	.310	-2.7	CF(59): 2.1	0.7
2021 FS	SD	MLB	24	600	105	.301	0.6	CF 3, LF 0	2.5
2021 DC	SD	MLB	24	617	105	.301	0.7	CF 3	2.8

Trent Grisham, continued

Batted Ball Distribution

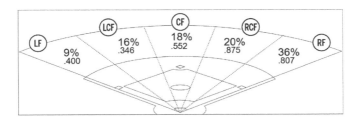

Strike Zone vs LHP   *Strike Zone vs RHP*

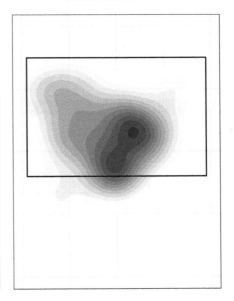

Eric Hosmer 1B

Born: 10/24/89   Age: 31   Bats: L   Throws: L
Height: 6'4"   Weight: 226   Origin: Round 1, 2008 Draft (#3 overall)

YEAR	TEAM	LVL	AGE	PA	R	2B	3B	HR	RBI	BB	K	SB	CS	AVG/OBP/SLG
2018	SD	MLB	28	677	72	31	2	18	69	62	142	7	4	.253/.322/.398
2019	SD	MLB	29	667	72	29	2	22	99	40	163	0	3	.265/.310/.425
2020	SD	MLB	30	156	23	6	0	9	36	9	28	4	0	.287/.333/.517
2021 FS	SD	MLB	31	600	77	26	1	22	85	51	127	4	2	.269/.335/.449
2021 DC	SD	MLB	31	580	75	25	1	22	82	49	123	4	2	.269/.335/.449

Comparables: Eric Karros, Greg Walker, Jesus Guzman

Hosmer has benefited from the inverse of the perception issues that Manny Machado has suffered from. He is so well regarded among his peers and outsiders that people tend to believe that he is a better player than he is. Nowadays, front offices are generally smart enough not to put excess value on soft factors, but Hosmer bucked that trend to earn an eight-year, $144 million deal that looked like it was going south just two seasons in. Thankfully, he started hitting like 2017 Hosmer again before breaking his finger on September 7 on—of all things, a bunt attempt. (Say a little prayer for Dave Cameron, folks.) The biggest change for Hosmer in 2020 was putting the ball in the air a lot more frequently than in the past (34.2 percent versus 23.1 percent), which is something he had been urged to do for his entire career. If he keeps that up, who knows? Maybe reality will align with perception after all.

YEAR	TEAM	LVL	AGE	PA	DRC+	BABIP	BRR	FRAA	WARP
2018	SD	MLB	28	677	83	.302	-2.6	1B(157): 7.8	0.1
2019	SD	MLB	29	667	86	.323	-0.2	1B(157): -3.9	-0.6
2020	SD	MLB	30	156	110	.296	0.6	1B(32): -0.1	0.3
2021 FS	SD	MLB	31	600	112	.313	-0.5	1B 0	1.7
2021 DC	SD	MLB	31	580	112	.313	-0.5	1B 0	1.7

Eric Hosmer, continued

Batted Ball Distribution

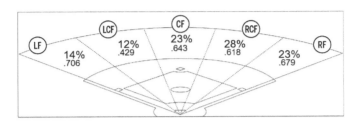

Strike Zone vs LHP

Strike Zone vs RHP

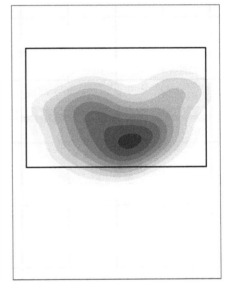

Manny Machado   3B

Born: 07/06/92   Age: 29   Bats: R   Throws: R
Height: 6'3"   Weight: 218   Origin: Round 1, 2010 Draft (#3 overall)

YEAR	TEAM	LVL	AGE	PA	R	2B	3B	HR	RBI	BB	K	SB	CS	AVG/OBP/SLG
2018	BAL	MLB	25	413	48	21	1	24	65	45	51	8	1	.315/.387/.575
2018	LAD	MLB	25	296	36	14	2	13	42	25	53	6	1	.273/.338/.487
2019	SD	MLB	26	661	81	21	2	32	85	65	128	5	3	.256/.334/.462
2020	SD	MLB	27	254	44	12	1	16	47	26	37	6	3	.304/.370/.580
2021 FS	SD	MLB	28	600	92	25	1	31	96	58	105	6	3	.272/.345/.507
2021 DC	SD	MLB	28	644	99	27	1	34	103	63	112	6	3	.272/.345/.507

Comparables: Casey McGehee, Ryan Zimmerman, Hank Blalock

One would have a hard time finding a player as talented and as unpopular as Machado is who lives outside of Houston (just imagine if he were an Astro) In his first full year in San Diego, those hoping for Machado to go bust got some hope. His offense was a far cry from what it was in 2018, and he didn't take well to a return to shortstop. Thankfully, the rise of Fernando Tatís Jr. allowed Machado to return to third. Not only did Machado become a defensive asset again, but he also started hitting like it was 2018. He pulled the ball more frequently and improved his plate discipline and contact rates, the latter of which was the difference between a 19.4 and 14.6 strikeout rate. His performance over a full season extrapolates to over six WARP, which would more than justify his contract and placement alongside the game's top players—even if he'll probably never receive the flowers he deserves from a fair chunk of the baseball world.

YEAR	TEAM	LVL	AGE	PA	DRC+	BABIP	BRR	FRAA	WARP
2018	BAL	MLB	25	413	141	.311	-0.5	SS(96): -4.5	3.5
2018	LAD	MLB	25	296	141	.296	1.4	SS(51): -4.5, 3B(16): 3.1	2.8
2019	SD	MLB	26	661	106	.274	-1.3	3B(119): -10.4, SS(37): -5.2	1.5
2020	SD	MLB	27	254	140	.297	-0.2	3B(56): 4.8	2.1
2021 FS	SD	MLB	28	600	131	.282	-0.3	3B 0, SS 0	3.8
2021 DC	SD	MLB	28	644	131	.282	-0.3	3B 0	3.7

Manny Machado, continued

Batted Ball Distribution

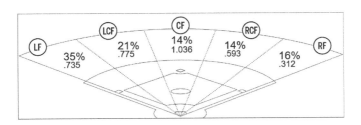

Strike Zone vs LHP   ## Strike Zone vs RHP

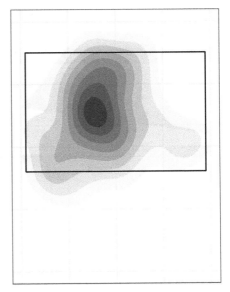

Mitch Moreland   1B

Born: 09/06/85   Age: 35   Bats: L   Throws: L
Height: 6'3"   Weight: 245   Origin: Round 17, 2007 Draft (#530 overall)

YEAR	TEAM	LVL	AGE	PA	R	2B	3B	HR	RBI	BB	K	SB	CS	AVG/OBP/SLG
2018	BOS	MLB	32	459	57	23	4	15	68	50	102	2	0	.245/.325/.433
2019	BOS	MLB	33	335	48	17	1	19	58	34	74	1	0	.252/.328/.507
2020	BOS	MLB	34	79	14	4	0	8	21	11	18	0	0	.328/.430/.746
2020	SD	MLB	34	73	8	5	0	2	8	4	14	0	0	.203/.247/.362
2021 FS	SD	MLB	35	600	69	24	1	25	78	55	149	1	1	.228/.306/.424
2021 DC	SD	MLB	35	447	52	18	1	19	58	41	111	0	1	.228/.306/.424

Comparables: Dae-Ho Lee, Garrett Jones, Andres Galarraga

   Moreland was one of the top hitters available at the deadline, a statement that says as much about the marketplace as it does about him and his hot first half. Unfortunately, he couldn't maintain his pace after shipping out west. Moreland's plate discipline took a dive after the trade and he started pressing more at the plate. The Padres were unimpressed, to the extent that they declined the same club option that appeared to be a gimme at the midway point. Moreland should, nevertheless, find work elsewhere as a platoon first baseman.

YEAR	TEAM	LVL	AGE	PA	DRC+	BABIP	BRR	FRAA	WARP
2018	BOS	MLB	32	459	102	.288	-2.5	1B(116): 2.4	0.8
2019	BOS	MLB	33	335	111	.271	-2.6	1B(85): 4.3	1.2
2020	BOS	MLB	34	79	120	.341	0.1	1B(22): -0.1	0.3
2020	SD	MLB	34	73	116	.226	-0.4	1B(16): -2.0	0.0
2021 FS	SD	MLB	35	600	99	.266	-0.8	1B 0	0.7
2021 DC	SD	MLB	35	447	99	.266	-0.6	1B 0	0.6

Mitch Moreland, continued

Batted Ball Distribution

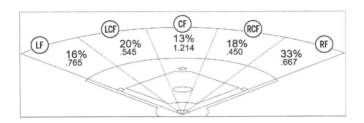

Strike Zone vs LHP   Strike Zone vs RHP

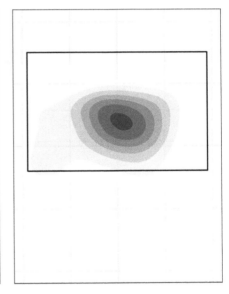

Wil Myers   LF

Born: 12/10/90   Age: 30   Bats: R   Throws: R
Height: 6'3"   Weight: 207   Origin: Round 3, 2009 Draft (#91 overall)

YEAR	TEAM	LVL	AGE	PA	R	2B	3B	HR	RBI	BB	K	SB	CS	AVG/OBP/SLG
2018	SD	MLB	27	343	39	25	1	11	39	30	94	13	1	.253/.318/.446
2019	SD	MLB	28	490	58	22	1	18	53	51	168	16	7	.239/.321/.418
2020	SD	MLB	29	218	34	14	2	15	40	18	56	2	1	.288/.353/.606
2021 FS	SD	MLB	30	600	81	25	2	28	86	60	170	19	7	.245/.323/.460
2021 DC	SD	MLB	30	562	76	23	1	26	80	56	159	18	6	.245/.323/.460

Comparables: Mike Jacobs, Adam LaRoche, Ike Davis

Myers' career has been marred by inconsistency in performance, in position, in reputation. It's jarring to realize he's only entering his age-30 season—it seems that time flies when you (and everyone else) can't decide if you're a replacement-level albatross or something a little more valuable. Myers was the latter in 2020. He posted the best DRC+ of his career, and did so without being forced to play a position that was beyond his reach, like center or third base. Indeed, he had the kind of year that everyone envisioned he would have when he was a young buck. The Padres, who owe him another $45 million, hope he can have a few more of those now that he's an older buck.

YEAR	TEAM	LVL	AGE	PA	DRC+	BABIP	BRR	FRAA	WARP
2018	SD	MLB	27	343	90	.327	1.3	3B(36): -4.3, LF(31): 0.8, RF(10): 1.4	0.6
2019	SD	MLB	28	490	84	.344	-1.6	LF(98): -2.8, CF(66): -1.1, 1B(7): -0.3	0.0
2020	SD	MLB	29	218	138	.331	1.9	RF(52): 1.0, 1B(2): -0.1	1.8
2021 FS	SD	MLB	30	600	116	.301	1.3	RF 3, 1B -1	3.1
2021 DC	SD	MLB	30	562	116	.301	1.2	RF 3, 1B -1	2.6

Wil Myers, continued

Batted Ball Distribution

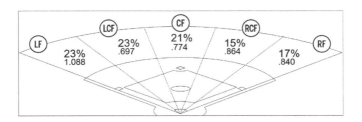

Strike Zone vs LHP

Strike Zone vs RHP

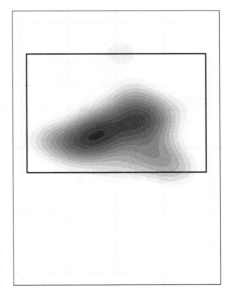

Austin Nola   C

Born: 12/28/89   Age: 31   Bats: R   Throws: R
Height: 6'0"   Weight: 197   Origin: Round 5, 2012 Draft (#167 overall)

YEAR	TEAM	LVL	AGE	PA	R	2B	3B	HR	RBI	BB	K	SB	CS	AVG/OBP/SLG
2018	NO	AAA	28	262	26	16	0	2	32	27	43	2	0	.279/.370/.376
2019	TAC	AAA	29	229	36	15	1	7	37	29	40	4	1	.327/.415/.520
2019	SEA	MLB	29	267	37	12	1	10	31	23	63	1	0	.269/.342/.454
2020	SEA	MLB	30	110	15	5	1	5	19	9	17	0	0	.306/.373/.531
2020	SD	MLB	30	74	9	4	0	2	9	9	17	0	0	.222/.324/.381
2021 FS	SD	MLB	31	600	72	26	1	16	72	53	131	0	1	.241/.317/.388
2021 DC	SD	MLB	31	473	57	20	1	13	56	42	103	0	1	.241/.317/.388

Comparables: Brian Daubach, Adam LaRoche, Paul Sorrento

Nola, part of the Padres' haul from the Mariners at the trade deadline, took the spot vacated by Austin Hedges, who was sent to Cleveland in a separate deal. Aaron's older brother is a late bloomer, having converted to catcher when he was 27 years old. Perhaps predictably, Nola is the inverse of Hedges: he's a bat-first backstop whose mitt is tolerable, but not exceptional. Baseball analysis is built on precedent, and there's precious little of that for this kind of career arc. As such, it's hard to have confidence that Nola will continue to be one of the game's best-hitting catchers heading into his age-31 season. The Padres don't have much to lose, though, and Nola deserves the opportunity to keep going for as long as he can.

YEAR	TEAM	LVL	AGE	PA	DRC+	BABIP	BRR	FRAA	WARP
2018	NO	AAA	28	262	111	.333	-2.2	C(68): 6.2	1.7
2019	TAC	AAA	29	229	119	.377	-3.4	C(28): 2.8, 1B(24): -0.8, 3B(3): 0.3	1.2
2019	SEA	MLB	29	267	101	.325	-0.5	1B(59): 2.4, 2B(15): 1.0, C(7): 0.4	0.9
2020	SEA	MLB	30	110	118	.325	-0.6	C(27): -0.1, 1B(2): 0.2, 3B(1): 0.0	0.8
2020	SD	MLB	30	74	119	.267	0.7	C(17): 0.3	0.6
2021 FS	SD	MLB	31	600	97	.287	-0.9	C 7, 1B 0	2.3
2021 DC	SD	MLB	31	473	97	.287	-0.7	C 7	2.4

Austin Nola, continued

Batted Ball Distribution

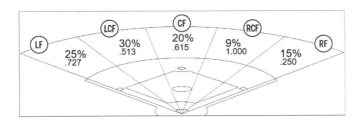

Strike Zone vs LHP   **Strike Zone vs RHP**

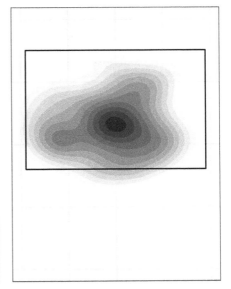

Tommy Pham   LF

Born: 03/08/88   Age: 33   Bats: R   Throws: R
Height: 6'1"   Weight: 223   Origin: Round 16, 2006 Draft (#496 overall)

YEAR	TEAM	LVL	AGE	PA	R	2B	3B	HR	RBI	BB	K	SB	CS	AVG/OBP/SLG
2018	STL	MLB	30	396	67	11	0	14	41	42	97	10	6	.248/.331/.399
2018	TB	MLB	30	174	35	7	6	7	22	25	43	5	1	.343/.448/.622
2019	TB	MLB	31	654	77	33	2	21	68	81	123	25	4	.273/.369/.450
2020	SD	MLB	32	125	13	2	0	3	12	15	27	6	0	.211/.312/.312
2021 FS	SD	MLB	33	600	81	23	1	20	75	73	153	19	7	.248/.347/.417
2021 DC	SD	MLB	33	593	80	22	1	19	74	73	151	18	7	.248/.347/.417

Comparables: Jason Bay, Kirk Gibson, Justin Upton

The phamtastic Pham was the headliner in the trade that also brought Cronenworth to town, though you wouldn't get that impression by looking at their statlines. Indeed, they more or less swapped the offensive performances that projections and analysts alike expected them to have. Pham's rough season can be blamed on his health. He tested positive for COVID-19 in July, then missed a month of the season because of a broken bone in his left hand. This offseason he was stabbed—one of those cases, evidently, of being at the wrong strip club at the wrong time. Given his track record, he should be a bounce-back candidate in 2021—right in time for his walk year.

YEAR	TEAM	LVL	AGE	PA	DRC+	BABIP	BRR	FRAA	WARP
2018	STL	MLB	30	396	121	.303	3.8	CF(91): -5.1	2.3
2018	TB	MLB	30	174	121	.442	0.9	LF(37): -0.5, CF(3): -0.2	0.9
2019	TB	MLB	31	654	115	.316	-0.2	LF(123): -9.6	2.0
2020	SD	MLB	32	125	91	.253	0.1	LF(18): -0.6	0.1
2021 FS	SD	MLB	33	600	114	.311	1.0	LF -1, CF 0	2.8
2021 DC	SD	MLB	33	593	114	.311	1.0	LF -1	2.3

Tommy Pham, continued

Batted Ball Distribution

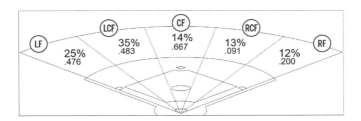

Strike Zone vs LHP   Strike Zone vs RHP

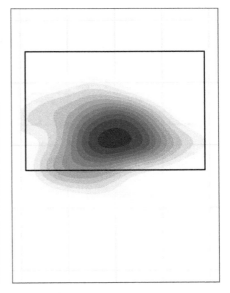

Jurickson Profar   LF

Born: 02/20/93   Age: 28   Bats: S   Throws: R
Height: 6'0"   Weight: 184   Origin: International Free Agent, 2009

YEAR	TEAM	LVL	AGE	PA	R	2B	3B	HR	RBI	BB	K	SB	CS	AVG/OBP/SLG
2018	TEX	MLB	25	594	82	35	6	20	77	54	88	10	0	.254/.335/.458
2019	OAK	MLB	26	518	65	24	2	20	67	48	75	9	1	.218/.301/.410
2020	SD	MLB	27	202	28	6	0	7	25	15	28	7	1	.278/.343/.428
2021 FS	SD	MLB	28	600	79	25	2	19	75	56	101	5	2	.250/.332/.420
2021 DC	SD	MLB	28	378	50	15	1	12	47	35	63	3	2	.250/.332/.420

Comparables: D'Angelo Jimenez, Ted Lepcio, Ray Durham

After a disappointing year in Oakland, Profar found salvation in San Diego in the company of two longtime admirers, Preller and Tingler. Not only did he have one of his best offensive seasons, he expanded his (at-times shaky) defensive role by splitting time between left field and second base. Profar is never going to live up to the star potential he was believed to have as a prospect, but he's hitting the free-agent market after having played in nearly 90 percent of his teams' games over the last three seasons and he should find a starting role for his age-28 season.

YEAR	TEAM	LVL	AGE	PA	DRC+	BABIP	BRR	FRAA	WARP
2018	TEX	MLB	25	594	109	.269	2.2	SS(68): -8.6, 3B(51): -3.7, 1B(24): 0.3	1.8
2019	OAK	MLB	26	518	96	.218	0.4	2B(124): -12.5, LF(7): 0.0, 1B(1): -0.0	0.2
2020	SD	MLB	27	202	104	.293	2.0	LF(36): -2.4, 2B(17): -3.5, RF(2): 0.2	0.3
2021 FS	SD	MLB	28	600	109	.273	-0.2	LF -1, RF 3	2.4
2021 DC	SD	MLB	28	378	109	.273	-0.1	LF -1, RF 2	1.4

Jurickson Profar, continued

Batted Ball Distribution

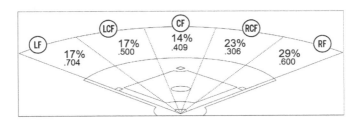

Strike Zone vs LHP   ## *Strike Zone vs RHP*

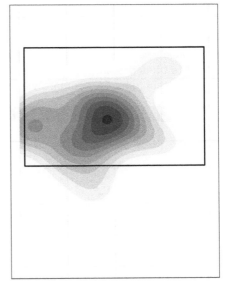

Fernando Tatís Jr. SS

Born: 01/02/99   Age: 22   Bats: R   Throws: R
Height: 6'3"   Weight: 217   Origin: International Free Agent, 2015

YEAR	TEAM	LVL	AGE	PA	R	2B	3B	HR	RBI	BB	K	SB	CS	AVG/OBP/SLG
2018	SA	AA	19	394	77	22	4	16	43	33	109	16	5	.286/.355/.507
2019	SD	MLB	20	372	61	13	6	22	53	30	110	16	6	.317/.379/.590
2020	SD	MLB	21	257	50	11	2	17	45	27	61	11	3	.277/.366/.571
2021 FS	SD	MLB	22	600	95	24	4	31	81	50	165	17	8	.263/.331/.499
2021 DC	SD	MLB	22	628	100	25	4	32	85	53	173	19	8	.263/.331/.499

Comparables: Darryl Strawberry, Bo Bichette, Ronald Acuña Jr.

Hey, did you know Tatís' father once hit two grand slams in an—we're kidding, we're kidding. Tatís has more than earned the right to stop sharing the stage with his old man, even if that fun fact will never die—broadcasters were still harping on Mike Piazza's being a 62nd-round draft pick when he was pushing 40. In 2020, Tatis continued his metamorphosis from top prospect to top player. He was never going to sustain his .410 BABIP of 2019, but he altered his game to adjust for that, making significant improvements to his strikeout and walk rates. He hit the ball harder, too—much, much harder. According to Statcast, Tatis had a league-leading 96.1 mph exit velocity in 2020, as compared to 90.4 mph in 2019. As for defense, the only way Tatís is going to win a Gold Glove is with his bat, but he did a better job of syncing his internal clock and there's no reason to think he's sliding off the six spot anytime soon. At just 21 years old, he seems certain to be a perennial MVP candidate.

YEAR	TEAM	LVL	AGE	PA	DRC+	BABIP	BRR	FRAA	WARP
2018	SA	AA	19	394	136	.370	3.0	SS(83): -1.9	2.4
2019	SD	MLB	20	372	118	.410	7.1	SS(83): 0.9	3.4
2020	SD	MLB	21	257	126	.306	0.7	SS(57): -5.5	0.9
2021 FS	SD	MLB	22	600	126	.318	1.7	SS -1	3.9
2021 DC	SD	MLB	22	628	126	.318	1.8	SS -1	4.0

Fernando Tatis Jr., continued

Batted Ball Distribution

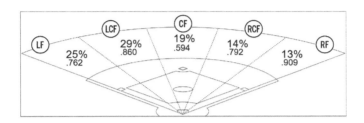

Strike Zone vs LHP   ## *Strike Zone vs RHP*

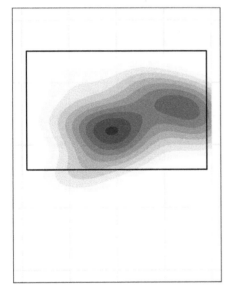   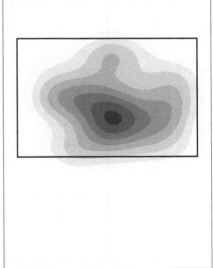

Dan Altavilla   RHP

Born: 09/08/92   Age: 28   Bats: R   Throws: R
Height: 5'11"   Weight: 226   Origin: Round 5, 2014 Draft (#141 overall)

YEAR	TEAM	LVL	AGE	W	L	SV	G	GS	IP	H	HR	BB/9	K/9	K	GB%	BABIP
2018	TAC	AAA	25	0	2	0	9	1	6²	9	2	5.4	9.4	7	34.8%	.333
2018	SEA	MLB	25	3	2	0	22	0	20²	11	2	6.5	10.0	23	37.8%	.209
2019	ARK	AA	26	3	0	4	14	0	16¹	7	1	1.7	13.8	25	41.9%	.200
2019	TAC	AAA	26	2	1	0	14	0	14	11	0	7.1	16.1	25	48.1%	.407
2019	SEA	MLB	26	2	1	0	17	0	14²	9	1	7.4	11.0	18	44.1%	.250
2020	SD	MLB	27	2	3	1	22	0	20¹	18	3	5.3	10.6	24	34.0%	.300
2021 FS	*SD*	*MLB*	*28*	*2*	*2*	*0*	*57*	*0*	*50*	*40*	*7*	*5.2*	*11.3*	*62*	*38.7%*	*.285*
2021 DC	*SD*	*MLB*	*28*	*2*	*2*	*0*	*50*	*0*	*41*	*33*	*5*	*5.2*	*11.3*	*51*	*38.7%*	*.285*

Comparables: Dominic Leone, Phil Maton, Keone Kela

After Altavilla arrived in San Diego as part of the Austin Nola trade, he had himself a nice little September. It's hard to draw a greater conclusion than this: He's the same pitcher he has been for years. He still has trouble finding the strike zone, like Luis Perdomo, but, unlike Perdomo, he doesn't strike out enough hitters to make him anything more than a back-end reliever.

YEAR	TEAM	LVL	AGE	WHIP	ERA	DRA-	WARP	MPH	FB%	WHF	CSP
2018	TAC	AAA	25	1.95	9.45	56	0.2				
2018	SEA	MLB	25	1.26	2.61	77	0.4	98.3	53.1%	32.0%	
2019	ARK	AA	26	0.61	1.10	37	0.6				
2019	TAC	AAA	26	1.57	8.36	57	0.5				
2019	SEA	MLB	26	1.43	5.52	93	0.1	98.6	59.3%	26.6%	
2020	SD	MLB	27	1.48	5.75	110	0.1	99.2	46.8%	31.6%	
2021 FS	*SD*	*MLB*	*28*	*1.39*	*4.15*	*94*	*0.4*	*98.9*	*51.4%*	*30.3%*	*46.1%*
2021 DC	*SD*	*MLB*	*28*	*1.39*	*4.15*	*94*	*0.3*	*98.9*	*51.4%*	*30.3%*	*46.1%*

Dan Altavilla, continued

Pitch Shape vs LHH

Pitch Shape vs RHH

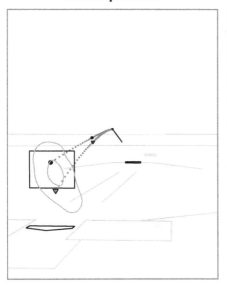
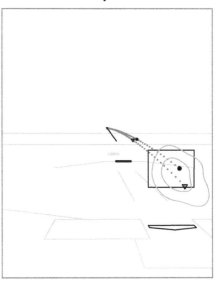

Type	Frequency	Velocity	H Movement	V Movement
● Fastball	46.6%	97.4 [115]	-8.2 [93]	-12.7 [107]
▽ Slider	52.1%	90.1 [127]	1 [84]	-23.9 [128]

Mike Clevinger RHP

Born: 12/21/90   Age: 30   Bats: R   Throws: R
Height: 6'4"   Weight: 215   Origin: Round 4, 2011 Draft (#135 overall)

YEAR	TEAM	LVL	AGE	W	L	SV	G	GS	IP	H	HR	BB/9	K/9	K	GB%	BABIP
2018	CLE	MLB	27	13	8	0	32	32	200	164	21	3.0	9.3	207	40.3%	.280
2019	CLE	MLB	28	13	4	0	21	21	126	96	10	2.6	12.1	169	40.5%	.306
2020	SD	MLB	29	3	2	0	8	8	41²	34	6	3.0	8.6	40	33.6%	.277
2021 FS	SD	MLB	30	2	2	0	57	0	50	43	7	3.4	10.3	57	37.6%	.287

Comparables: Kevin Gausman, Anthony DeSclafani, Zack Wheeler

Clevinger arrived in San Diego from Cleveland as part of a nine-player swap that crowned the team's busy deadline. He was excellent in his four starts after the trade, but it's been downhill since,and not in the good, easy-breezy way. A strained elbow limited Clevinger to a single inning in the postseason, and he underwent Tommy John surgery early in the offseason, wiping out his 2021. Both the Padres and Clevinger will have a lot riding on his 2022 season—the former hoping he justifies the trade, the latter needing a good performance to ensure a quality free-agent contract after that year.

YEAR	TEAM	LVL	AGE	WHIP	ERA	DRA-	WARP	MPH	FB%	WHF	CSP
2018	CLE	MLB	27	1.16	3.02	78	4.1	96.0	52.9%	27.9%	
2019	CLE	MLB	28	1.06	2.71	68	3.3	97.5	51.1%	35.3%	
2020	SD	MLB	29	1.15	3.02	105	0.3	97.0	46.8%	30.4%	
2021 FS	SD	MLB	30	1.24	3.57	85	0.7	96.9	50.9%	31.7%	47.3%

Mike Clevinger, continued

Pitch Shape vs LHH

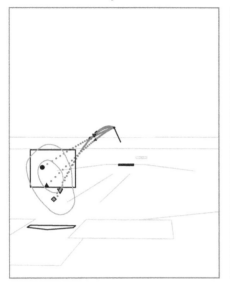

Pitch Shape vs RHH

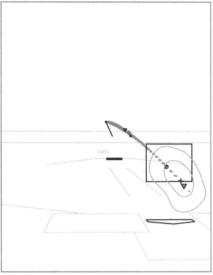

Type	Frequency	Velocity	H Movement	V Movement
● Fastball	39.9%	95.2 [108]	-6.2 [102]	-11.2 [111]
+ Cutter	6.9%	88 [98]	3.7 [112]	-26.6 [91]
▲ Changeup	8.3%	87.4 [109]	-9.6 [111]	-21.2 [117]
▽ Slider	32.4%	81.7 [90]	12 [126]	-36.6 [92]
◇ Curveball	12.5%	78.8 [101]	3.4 [83]	-49 [99]

Yu Darvish RHP

Born: 08/16/86 Age: 34 Bats: R Throws: R
Height: 6'5" Weight: 220 Origin: International Free Agent, 2012

YEAR	TEAM	LVL	AGE	W	L	SV	G	GS	IP	H	HR	BB/9	K/9	K	GB%	BABIP
2018	SB	LO-A	31	0	0	0	2	2	6	4	1	1.5	9.0	6	37.5%	.200
2018	CHC	MLB	31	1	3	0	8	8	40	36	7	4.7	11.0	49	36.8%	.296
2019	CHC	MLB	32	6	8	0	31	31	178²	140	33	2.8	11.5	229	45.1%	.268
2020	CHC	MLB	33	8	3	0	12	12	76	59	5	1.7	11.0	93	42.8%	.297
2021 FS	SD	MLB	34	10	7	0	26	26	150	124	19	2.9	10.6	175	43.1%	.284
2021 DC	SD	MLB	34	11	8	0	29	29	169	139	21	2.9	10.6	198	43.1%	.284

Comparables: Max Scherzer, Corey Kluber, Carlos Carrasco

What is the difference between an overpaid disappointment and a Cy Young finalist? By DRA, Darvish was actually a better pitcher in 2019 than he was in the season in which he finished third in Cy Young voting. The biggest difference? That pesky gopherball. With the baseballs less juiced in 2020, Darvish's home run rate plummeted; everything else stayed as good as it ever was, and not in some lame, Toby Keith-ass way. Some of it even got better. Darvish cut his walk rate, starting throwing his breaking stuff far more often and reduced his fastball usage to a career-low 16.6 percent. Even more impressive, despite playing all of his games against the Central divisions, he didn't exactly do what he did against the dregs of the league: His final eight starts came against teams who finished with a winning record. All of that adds up to a pitcher who is exactly the type of ace many long believed he was, and who the Padres hope he will continue to be.

YEAR	TEAM	LVL	AGE	WHIP	ERA	DRA-	WARP	MPH	FB%	WHF	CSP
2018	SB	LO-A	31	0.83	1.50	92	0.1				
2018	CHC	MLB	31	1.43	4.95	105	0.3	96.2	69.1%	25.5%	
2019	CHC	MLB	32	1.10	3.98	55	6.0	96.7	39.8%	30.3%	
2020	CHC	MLB	33	0.96	2.01	67	2.0	97.6	30.1%	32.2%	
2021 FS	SD	MLB	34	1.15	3.10	76	3.4	97.0	38.6%	30.6%	49.4%
2021 DC	SD	MLB	34	1.15	3.10	76	3.9	97.0	38.6%	30.6%	49.4%

Yu Darvish, continued

Pitch Shape vs LHH

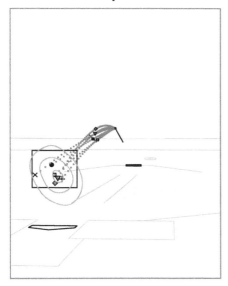

Pitch Shape vs RHH

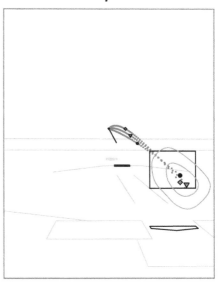

Type	Frequency	Velocity	H Movement	V Movement
● Fastball	15.5%	96.1 [111]	-5.5 [106]	-10.3 [114]
□ Sinker	9.5%	95 [113]	-12.4 [105]	-16.5 [113]
+ Cutter	5.0%	92.5 [126]	2 [100]	-17.8 [125]
✕ Splitter	5.1%	90.6 [125]	-4.4 [113]	-24.7 [116]
▽ Slider	46.1%	85.4 [107]	7.1 [107]	-34.4 [98]
◇ Curveball	15.4%	78.9 [101]	9.6 [108]	-49.4 [98]

Javy Guerra   RHP

Born: 09/25/95   Age: 25   Bats: L   Throws: R
Height: 6'0"   Weight: 185   Origin: International Free Agent, 2012

YEAR	TEAM	LVL	AGE	W	L	SV	G	GS	IP	H	HR	BB/9	K/9	K	GB%	BABIP
2019	LE	HI-A	23	0	0	1	17	0	17	13	2	2.6	12.2	23	34.2%	.306
2019	SD	MLB	23	0	0	0	8	0	8²	7	3	3.1	6.2	6	48.1%	.167
2020	SD	MLB	24	1	0	0	14	0	13¹	25	1	3.4	8.1	12	51.0%	.500
2021 FS	SD	MLB	25	2	2	0	57	0	50	47	7	3.3	8.3	46	45.3%	.287
2021 DC	SD	MLB	25	1	1	0	33	0	41	39	5	3.3	8.3	38	45.3%	.287

Once a promising shortstop prospect, Guerra's inability to hit and strong arm led to him hopping on the mound before the 2019 season. He was shockingly effective for a newcomer, though his upper-90s sinker-slider combo with the occasional changeup mixed in hasn't yet led to success in the majors. Guerra's backstory is unusual,but his profile is ubiquitous. Given that essential fungibility the Padres will likely keep him on a short leash.

YEAR	TEAM	LVL	AGE	WHIP	ERA	DRA-	WARP	MPH	FB%	WHF	CSP
2019	LE	HI-A	23	1.06	3.71	75	0.2				
2019	SD	MLB	23	1.15	5.19	125	-0.1	99.9	76.9%	17.2%	
2020	SD	MLB	24	2.25	10.12	86	0.2	100.3	68.1%	21.2%	
2021 FS	SD	MLB	25	1.31	4.04	96	0.4	100.2	70.5%	20.1%	50.5%
2021 DC	SD	MLB	25	1.31	4.04	96	0.3	100.2	70.5%	20.1%	50.5%

Javy Guerra, continued

Pitch Shape vs LHH

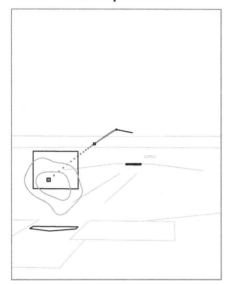

Pitch Shape vs RHH

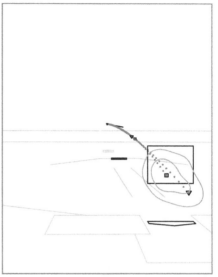

Type	Frequency	Velocity	H Movement	V Movement
● Fastball	7.2%	98.4 [118]	-11.2 [79]	-13.9 [104]
□ Sinker	60.9%	98.5 [131]	-14.5 [90]	-16.9 [112]
▲ Changeup	4.7%	91.9 [126]	-13.1 [93]	-22 [115]
▽ Slider	27.2%	87.9 [118]	4.6 [97]	-29.6 [112]

Tim Hill LHP

Born: 02/10/90   Age: 31   Bats: R   Throws: L
Height: 6'4"   Weight: 200   Origin: Round 32, 2014 Draft (#963 overall)

YEAR	TEAM	LVL	AGE	W	L	SV	G	GS	IP	H	HR	BB/9	K/9	K	GB%	BABIP
2018	KC	MLB	28	1	4	2	70	0	45²	46	4	2.8	8.3	42	60.7%	.313
2019	OMA	AAA	29	1	1	3	27	0	29²	26	2	1.8	9.1	30	55.0%	.308
2019	KC	MLB	29	2	0	1	46	0	39²	31	4	2.9	8.8	39	56.2%	.270
2020	SD	MLB	30	3	0	0	23	0	18	17	3	3.0	10.0	20	52.9%	.292
2021 FS	SD	MLB	31	2	2	0	57	0	50	45	5	2.6	8.9	49	53.9%	.293
2021 DC	SD	MLB	31	2	2	0	50	0	47	43	4	2.6	8.9	46	53.9%	.293

Comparables: Adam Kolarek, Josh Osich, Nick Ramirez

The Royals traded Hill to the Padres before the season, perhaps because they suspected he would be unable to repeat his 2019 with the three-batter-minimum in place. The Royals were right, but Hill remains an effective left-on-left reliever who can provide value with some careful micromanagement.

YEAR	TEAM	LVL	AGE	WHIP	ERA	DRA-	WARP	MPH	FB%	WHF	CSP
2018	KC	MLB	28	1.31	4.53	111	0.0	93.1	76.4%	19.7%	
2019	OMA	AAA	29	1.08	2.12	44	1.2				
2019	KC	MLB	29	1.11	3.63	74	0.7	92.0	75.5%	20.7%	
2020	SD	MLB	30	1.28	4.50	81	0.3	92.8	89.9%	22.8%	
2021 FS	SD	MLB	31	1.20	3.30	81	0.8	92.6	80.6%	21.2%	52.4%
2021 DC	SD	MLB	31	1.20	3.30	81	0.7	92.6	80.6%	21.2%	52.4%

Tim Hill, continued

Pitch Shape vs LHH

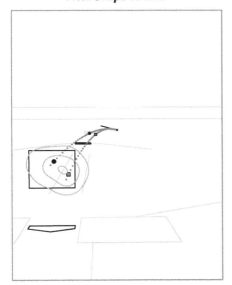

Pitch Shape vs RHH

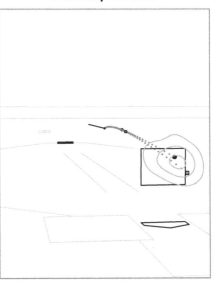

Type	Frequency	Velocity	H Movement	V Movement
● Fastball	45.7%	91.5 [96]	16.6 [53]	-26.1 [69]
□ Sinker	43.7%	89.7 [86]	15.4 [83]	-34.5 [55]
▽ Slider	10.0%	80.3 [84]	0.8 [77]	-35 [96]

Pierce Johnson RHP

Born: 05/10/91   Age: 30   Bats: R   Throws: R
Height: 6'2"   Weight: 202   Origin: Round 1, 2012 Draft (#43 overall)

YEAR	TEAM	LVL	AGE	W	L	SV	G	GS	IP	H	HR	BB/9	K/9	K	GB%	BABIP
2018	SAC	AAA	27	0	0	4	17	0	22²	15	1	4.0	11.9	30	32.7%	.275
2018	SF	MLB	27	3	2	0	37	0	43²	38	5	4.5	7.4	36	39.1%	.270
2020	SD	MLB	29	3	1	0	24	0	20	15	2	4.0	12.2	27	31.8%	.310
2021 FS	SD	MLB	30	2	2	0	57	0	50	39	6	3.8	11.6	64	37.0%	.285
2021 DC	SD	MLB	30	2	2	0	50	0	47	37	6	3.8	11.6	60	37.0%	.285

Comparables: Hansel Robles, Dylan Floro, Mike Morin

Johnson had forgettable big-league stints with the Cubs and Giants before heading overseas for a season with the Hanshin Tigers. That turned out to be a worthwhile detour for him, as he posted a 1.38 ERA and a 7.00 strikeout-to-walk ratio in 58 appearances, a performance which, in turn, persuaded the Padres to hand over a multi-year deal worth $5 million. Johnson delivered in year one, working around walks to strike out over a third of the batters he faced. Another season like that and the Padres will assuredly exercise their $3 million club option for 2022.

YEAR	TEAM	LVL	AGE	WHIP	ERA	DRA-	WARP	MPH	FB%	WHF	CSP
2018	SAC	AAA	27	1.10	3.57	67	0.5				
2018	SF	MLB	27	1.37	5.56	112	-0.1	95.3	50.2%	24.5%	
2020	SD	MLB	29	1.20	2.70	87	0.3	97.6	45.8%	40.0%	
2021 FS	SD	MLB	30	1.22	3.41	81	0.8	96.5	47.9%	32.7%	46.3%
2021 DC	SD	MLB	30	1.22	3.41	81	0.7	96.5	47.9%	32.7%	46.3%

Pierce Johnson, continued

| | **Pitch Shape vs LHH** | | | **Pitch Shape vs RHH** |

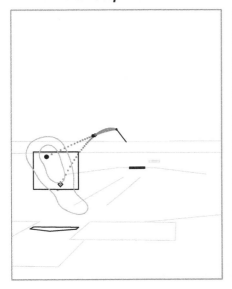 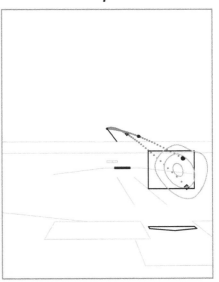

Type	Frequency	Velocity	H Movement	V Movement
● Fastball	45.8%	96.3 [112]	-9.2 [88]	-12.6 [107]
◇ Curveball	54.2%	84.7 [124]	11.8 [117]	-38.7 [122]

Dinelson Lamet   RHP

Born: 07/18/92   Age: 28   Bats: R   Throws: R
Height: 6'3"   Weight: 228   Origin: International Free Agent, 2014

YEAR	TEAM	LVL	AGE	W	L	SV	G	GS	IP	H	HR	BB/9	K/9	K	GB%	BABIP
2019	LE	HI-A	26	0	2	0	3	3	9	11	1	5.0	14.0	14	27.3%	.476
2019	ELP	AAA	26	1	0	0	3	3	15	10	3	2.4	11.4	19	51.4%	.219
2019	SD	MLB	26	3	5	0	14	14	73	62	12	3.7	12.9	105	35.3%	.314
2020	SD	MLB	27	3	1	0	12	12	69	39	5	2.6	12.1	93	38.0%	.234
2021 FS	SD	MLB	28	10	7	0	26	26	150	118	22	3.8	11.9	198	38.1%	.284
2021 DC	SD	MLB	28	8	6	0	25	22	124.7	98	18	3.8	11.9	165	38.1%	.284

Comparables: Nick Pivetta, Luis Castillo, Jon Gray

Lamet's season might have eliminated any fear that he'd end up in the bullpen. He cut his run average roughly in half, continued to strike out over a third of the batters he faced and lowered his walk rate by two percentage points, thus achieving a better-than-average rate for the first time in his major-league career. One significant change Lamet made was to use his sinker—a pitch that has fallen more and more out of favor league-wide during the launch-angle revolution era—less than ever. In its place, he relied more on his four-seamer and slider. Regression is likely in 2021, but that doesn't mean he can't be an impactful member of the starting rotation.

YEAR	TEAM	LVL	AGE	WHIP	ERA	DRA-	WARP	MPH	FB%	WHF	CSP
2019	LE	HI-A	26	1.78	8.00	127	-0.1				
2019	ELP	AAA	26	0.93	4.80	41	0.7				
2019	SD	MLB	26	1.26	4.07	65	2.0	97.8	54.8%	31.8%	
2020	SD	MLB	27	0.86	2.09	68	1.8	99.0	46.5%	32.6%	
2021 FS	SD	MLB	28	1.21	3.46	83	2.9	98.5	50.1%	32.2%	46.4%
2021 DC	SD	MLB	28	1.21	3.46	83	2.4	98.5	50.1%	32.2%	46.4%

Dinelson Lamet, continued

Pitch Shape vs LHH

Pitch Shape vs RHH

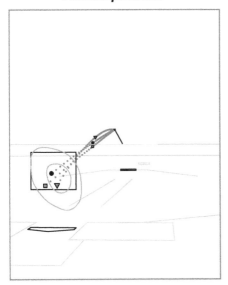
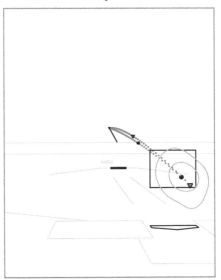

Type	Frequency	Velocity	H Movement	V Movement
● Fastball	41.2%	97 [114]	-5.8 [104]	-10.8 [112]
□ Sinker	5.3%	96.7 [122]	-12.3 [106]	-12.8 [125]
▽ Slider	53.4%	86.5 [111]	4.1 [96]	-31 [108]

Adrian Morejon   LHP

Born: 02/27/99   Age: 22   Bats: L   Throws: L
Height: 5'11"   Weight: 224   Origin: International Free Agent, 2016

YEAR	TEAM	LVL	AGE	W	L	SV	G	GS	IP	H	HR	BB/9	K/9	K	GB%	BABIP
2018	SD1	ROK	19	0	1	0	1	1	2²	5	0	0.0	13.5	4	44.4%	.556
2018	LE	HI-A	19	4	4	0	13	13	62²	54	6	3.4	10.1	70	51.5%	.306
2019	AMA	AA	20	0	4	0	16	16	36	29	3	3.8	11.0	44	48.9%	.292
2019	SD	MLB	20	0	0	0	5	2	8	15	1	3.4	10.1	9	36.7%	.483
2020	SD	MLB	21	2	2	0	9	4	19¹	20	7	1.9	11.6	25	46.0%	.302
2021 FS	SD	MLB	22	9	8	0	26	26	150	137	22	3.9	9.4	157	43.8%	.290
2021 DC	SD	MLB	22	6	5	0	33	11	77.7	71	11	3.9	9.4	81	43.8%	.290

Comparables: Luiz Gohara, Jesús Luzardo, Kolby Allard

Morejón recovered from a rough introduction to the majors in 2019, posting excellent strikeout and walk rates over a 19-inning sample. The wildest part of his year was his proclivity to give up the long ball. For context: Pitchers as a whole yielded home runs to 3.5 percent of the batters they faced; Morejón gave up a gopherball to 8.9 percent of the batters he faced. Obviously there's no reason to believe that will remain the case heading forward—pitchers with this kind of stuff don't yield more than three homers per nine on a true-talent basis. The more interesting subplot is whether the Padres return Morejón to a rotation or keep him in the bullpen because of his size and injury history.

YEAR	TEAM	LVL	AGE	WHIP	ERA	DRA-	WARP	MPH	FB%	WHF	CSP
2018	SD1	ROK	19	1.88	6.75						
2018	LE	HI-A	19	1.24	3.30	75	1.1				
2019	AMA	AA	20	1.22	4.25	56	1.0				
2019	SD	MLB	20	2.25	10.12	104	0.0	97.8	53.9%	19.7%	
2020	SD	MLB	21	1.24	4.66	88	0.3	98.2	56.2%	28.5%	
2021 FS	SD	MLB	22	1.36	4.22	98	1.6	98.1	55.7%	26.4%	47.3%
2021 DC	SD	MLB	22	1.36	4.22	98	0.7	98.1	55.7%	26.4%	47.3%

Adrian Morejon, continued

Pitch Shape vs LHH

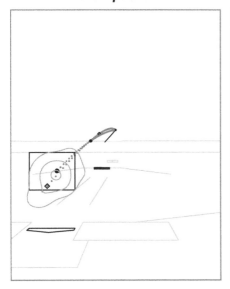

Pitch Shape vs RHH

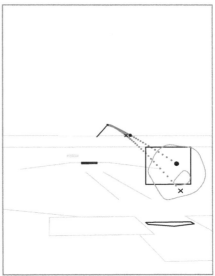

Type	Frequency	Velocity	H Movement	V Movement
● Fastball	56.2%	96.6 [113]	9.5 [87]	-13.8 [104]
✕ Splitter	17.4%	84.4 [96]	10.1 [92]	-29.8 [99]
▽ Slider	9.9%	85.6 [107]	-5.9 [102]	-35.1 [96]
◇ Curveball	16.5%	81.2 [110]	-12.2 [119]	-42.6 [113]

Joe Musgrove   RHP

Born: 12/04/92   Age: 28   Bats: R   Throws: R
Height: 6'5"   Weight: 230   Origin: Round 1, 2011 Draft (#46 overall)

YEAR	TEAM	LVL	AGE	W	L	SV	G	GS	IP	H	HR	BB/9	K/9	K	GB%	BABIP
2018	IND	AAA	25	1	1	0	2	2	10^2	10	0	1.7	9.3	11	37.5%	.312
2018	PIT	MLB	25	6	9	0	19	19	115^1	113	12	1.8	7.8	100	45.9%	.297
2019	PIT	MLB	26	11	12	0	32	31	170^1	168	21	2.1	8.3	157	44.1%	.300
2020	PIT	MLB	27	1	5	0	8	8	39^2	33	5	3.6	12.5	55	47.3%	.318
2021 FS	SD	MLB	28	10	7	0	26	26	150	134	20	2.4	9.8	164	44.5%	.292
2021 DC	SD	MLB	28	8	6	0	27	24	123.7	110	16	2.4	9.8	135	44.5%	.292

Comparables: Kevin Gausman, Jameson Taillon, Zach Davies

The one they call "Big Joe" wears a cornicello necklace, a pointy, twisted gold horn meant to protect one from the evil eye or anyone who wants to talk about the Gerrit Cole trade. Maybe Musgrove should take it in to get serviced, though, as he missed a third of this shortened season with triceps inflammation, perhaps caused by pointing to the sky at the four homers he served up in under 15 innings before the injury. Musgrove improved significantly upon his return from the IL, giving up a single long ball and setting a career-best mark for strikeout percentage. He's an excellent sleeper fantasy target in 2021, but approach with caution, as even his cornicello can't protect him from the trade winds in Pittsburgh.

YEAR	TEAM	LVL	AGE	WHIP	ERA	DRA-	WARP	MPH	FB%	WHF	CSP
2018	IND	AAA	25	1.12	5.06	67	0.3				
2018	PIT	MLB	25	1.18	4.06	76	2.5	95.2	50.3%	23.7%	
2019	PIT	MLB	26	1.22	4.44	73	4.0	94.8	49.5%	24.7%	
2020	PIT	MLB	27	1.24	3.86	73	0.9	94.5	39.1%	33.0%	
2021 FS	SD	MLB	28	1.16	3.31	82	3.0	94.8	47.3%	26.4%	49.1%
2021 DC	SD	MLB	28	1.16	3.31	82	2.5	94.8	47.3%	26.4%	49.1%

Joe Musgrove, continued

Pitch Shape vs LHH

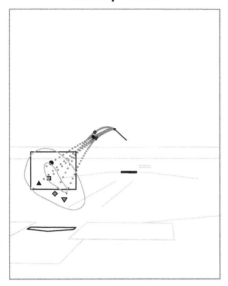

Pitch Shape vs RHH

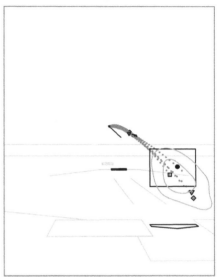

Type	Frequency	Velocity	H Movement	V Movement
● Fastball	27.0%	92.9 [101]	-5 [108]	-17 [95]
□ Sinker	12.0%	92.2 [99]	-10 [122]	-23.6 [90]
+ Cutter	5.9%	88.5 [101]	2.7 [105]	-25.1 [97]
▲ Changeup	10.8%	86.7 [106]	-11.5 [101]	-28.3 [98]
▽ Slider	24.2%	82.8 [95]	12 [126]	-37.3 [90]
◇ Curveball	19.9%	81.2 [110]	9.4 [108]	-48.8 [99]

Chris Paddack RHP

Born: 01/08/96   Age: 25   Bats: R   Throws: R
Height: 6'5"   Weight: 217   Origin: Round 8, 2015 Draft (#236 overall)

YEAR	TEAM	LVL	AGE	W	L	SV	G	GS	IP	H	HR	BB/9	K/9	K	GB%	BABIP
2018	LE	HI-A	22	4	1	0	10	10	52^1	43	3	0.7	14.3	83	43.2%	.374
2018	SA	AA	22	3	2	0	7	7	37^2	23	1	1.0	8.8	37	43.6%	.239
2019	SD	MLB	23	9	7	0	26	26	140^2	107	23	2.0	9.8	153	39.2%	.239
2020	SD	MLB	24	4	5	0	12	12	59	60	14	1.8	8.8	58	46.8%	.289
2021 FS	SD	MLB	25	10	7	0	26	26	150	128	19	2.1	9.4	156	44.1%	.278
2021 DC	SD	MLB	25	8	5	0	25	22	120	102	15	2.1	9.4	125	44.1%	.278

Comparables: Luis Severino, Shane Bieber, Aaron Nola

Paddack took a step back following a promising rookie season. He still excelled at limiting free passes, but his strikeout percentage dipped and he allowed more home runs on a rate basis. Paddack has been a two-pitch pitcher for the most part, leaning on his fastball-changeup combination. That approach didn't work so well last season, as opponents hit .308 against the heater. He did introduce a cutter during the season, and while the results weren't great, the development of that pitch could go a long way in helping him get back to good.

YEAR	TEAM	LVL	AGE	WHIP	ERA	DRA-	WARP	MPH	FB%	WHF	CSP
2018	LE	HI-A	22	0.90	2.24	45	1.9				
2018	SA	AA	22	0.72	1.91	58	1.1				
2019	SD	MLB	23	0.98	3.33	65	4.0	96.0	61.0%	24.8%	
2020	SD	MLB	24	1.22	4.73	97	0.6	96.1	61.6%	26.0%	
2021 FS	SD	MLB	25	1.08	2.91	74	3.6	96.0	61.2%	25.3%	50.0%
2021 DC	SD	MLB	25	1.08	2.91	74	2.9	96.0	61.2%	25.3%	50.0%

Chris Paddack, continued

Pitch Shape vs LHH

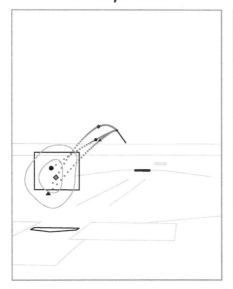

Pitch Shape vs RHH

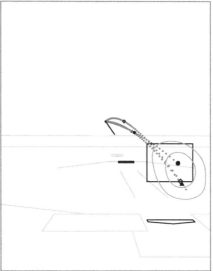

Type	Frequency	Velocity	H Movement	V Movement
● Fastball	58.0%	94.1 [105]	-8.6 [91]	-13.2 [106]
+ Cutter	3.5%	88 [98]	1.2 [95]	-25.8 [94]
▲ Changeup	31.0%	83.9 [95]	-12 [99]	-28.7 [97]
◇ Curveball	7.4%	76.9 [93]	5.5 [92]	-56.5 [82]

Emilio Pagán   RHP

Born: 05/07/91   Age: 30   Bats: L   Throws: R
Height: 6'2"   Weight: 208   Origin: Round 10, 2013 Draft (#297 overall)

YEAR	TEAM	LVL	AGE	W	L	SV	G	GS	IP	H	HR	BB/9	K/9	K	GB%	BABIP
2018	NAS	AAA	27	1	0	0	5	0	6	5	2	0.0	16.5	11	38.5%	.273
2018	OAK	MLB	27	3	1	0	55	0	62	55	13	2.8	9.1	63	25.4%	.256
2019	DUR	AAA	28	0	0	2	4	1	6	2	0	6.0	15.0	10	45.5%	.182
2019	TB	MLB	28	4	2	20	66	0	70	45	12	1.7	12.3	96	35.0%	.228
2020	SD	MLB	29	0	1	2	22	0	22	14	4	3.7	9.4	23	30.9%	.196
2021 FS	SD	MLB	30	3	2	13	57	0	50	38	7	2.7	10.8	59	30.8%	.260
2021 DC	SD	MLB	30	2	2	13	50	0	47	36	7	2.7	10.8	56	30.8%	.260

Comparables: Nick Wittgren, Paul Sewald, Ryan Dull

Pagán played on his fourth different team in as many years when the Rays traded him as part of the Manuel Margot deal. He was supposed to give the Padres yet another high-grade reliever. Alas, that isn't how things played out. His control faltered, leading to a walk rate that was nearly double his career rate going into the season, and he once again proved home-run prone. Pagán seems to have a Saberhagen-like tendency to alternate between good and bad years, so expect a rebound effort in 2021.

YEAR	TEAM	LVL	AGE	WHIP	ERA	DRA-	WARP	MPH	FB%	WHF	CSP
2018	NAS	AAA	27	0.83	3.00	30	0.3				
2018	OAK	MLB	27	1.19	4.35	97	0.4	95.7	66.4%	29.6%	
2019	DUR	AAA	28	1.00	0.00	35	0.3				
2019	TB	MLB	28	0.83	2.31	59	1.9	97.2	61.5%	35.1%	
2020	SD	MLB	29	1.05	4.50	111	0.1	96.1	62.4%	26.7%	
2021 FS	SD	MLB	30	1.06	2.87	72	1.0	96.6	62.9%	31.6%	49.2%
2021 DC	SD	MLB	30	1.06	2.87	72	1.0	96.6	62.9%	31.6%	49.2%

Emilio Pagán, continued

Pitch Shape vs LHH

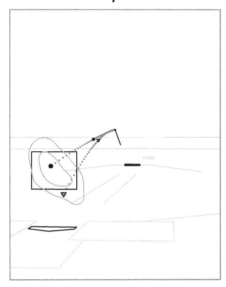

Pitch Shape vs RHH

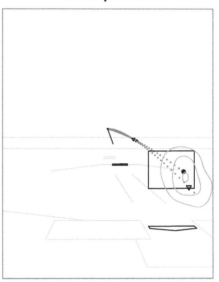

Type	Frequency	Velocity	H Movement	V Movement
● Fastball	62.4%	94.5 [106]	-4.8 [109]	-11.8 [110]
▽ Slider	37.6%	86.3 [110]	2.3 [89]	-30 [111]

Drew Pomeranz LHP

Born: 11/22/88   Age: 32   Bats: R   Throws: L
Height: 6'5"   Weight: 246   Origin: Round 1, 2010 Draft (#5 overall)

YEAR	TEAM	LVL	AGE	W	L	SV	G	GS	IP	H	HR	BB/9	K/9	K	GB%	BABIP
2018	WOR	AAA	29	0	2	0	5	5	19²	16	7	5.9	5.5	12	55.9%	.173
2018	BOS	MLB	29	2	6	0	26	11	74	87	12	5.4	8.0	66	37.8%	.344
2019	MIL	MLB	30	0	1	2	25	1	26¹	16	4	2.7	15.4	45	46.8%	.279
2019	SF	MLB	30	2	9	0	21	17	77²	89	17	4.2	10.7	92	36.3%	.353
2020	SD	MLB	31	1	0	4	20	0	18²	9	1	4.8	14.0	29	47.1%	.242
2021 FS	SD	MLB	32	2	2	18	57	0	50	43	6	4.5	11.0	61	41.1%	.297
2021 DC	SD	MLB	32	2	2	18	50	0	47	40	6	4.5	11.0	57	41.1%	.297

Comparables: Liam Hendriks, Tyler Thornburg, Alex Colomé

It's generally held as a bad idea to give a four-year contract to any reliever, even if they have a proven track record. Thus, the Padres were gambling when they handed a four-year pact to Pomeranz after he made 24 appearances in relief to close out the 2019 season. He was awesome for the Brewers, to be clear, but the rule of thumb is to pay for neither past production nor small-sample sizes. A year in, Pomeranz looks like the exception to all kinds of evaluative principles. He struck out nearly 40 percent of the batters he faced on the season, all but eliminated contact that wasn't of the groundball or pop-up variety, and didn't allow a run until his final appearance of the season. Pomeranz's elevated walk rate was the one blemish on his record, but, reread the previous sentence and try to feign concern.

YEAR	TEAM	LVL	AGE	WHIP	ERA	DRA-	WARP	MPH	FB%	WHF	CSP
2018	WOR	AAA	29	1.47	5.49	97	0.2				
2018	BOS	MLB	29	1.77	6.08	176	-2.3	91.6	58.9%	17.9%	
2019	MIL	MLB	30	0.91	2.39	10	1.6	96.1	76.5%	38.0%	
2019	SF	MLB	30	1.61	5.68	121	-0.2	94.2	63.8%	23.6%	
2020	SD	MLB	31	1.02	1.45	77	0.4	96.2	79.6%	34.7%	
2021 FS	SD	MLB	32	1.36	3.95	92	0.5	94.8	66.8%	26.1%	47.4%
2021 DC	SD	MLB	32	1.36	3.95	92	0.5	94.8	66.8%	26.1%	47.4%

Drew Pomeranz, continued

Pitch Shape vs LHH

Pitch Shape vs RHH

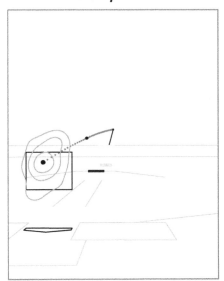
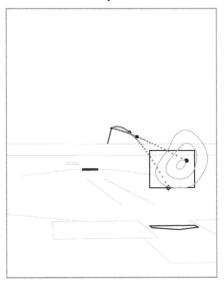

Type	Frequency	Velocity	H Movement	V Movement
● Fastball	79.6%	94.7 [107]	3.7 [114]	-10.8 [112]
◇ Curveball	20.4%	84.1 [121]	-3.3 [83]	-45.8 [106]

Trevor Rosenthal   RHP

Born: 05/29/90   Age: 31   Bats: R   Throws: R
Height: 6'2"   Weight: 230   Origin: Round 21, 2009 Draft (#639 overall)

YEAR	TEAM	LVL	AGE	W	L	SV	G	GS	IP	H	HR	BB/9	K/9	K	GB%	BABIP
2019	HBG	AA	29	0	1	0	10	0	9¹	9	2	6.8	10.6	11	46.2%	.292
2019	TOL	AAA	29	0	0	0	6	0	5¹	8	2	10.1	15.2	9	53.3%	.462
2019	WAS	MLB	29	0	1	0	12	0	6¹	8	0	21.3	7.1	5	35.0%	.400
2019	DET	MLB	29	0	0	0	10	0	9	3	0	11.0	12.0	12	50.0%	.176
2020	SD	MLB	30	1	0	11	23	0	23²	12	2	3.0	14.5	38	38.6%	.238
2021 FS	SD	MLB	31	2	2	26	57	0	50	39	5	5.5	12.0	66	42.7%	.296
2021 DC	SD	MLB	31	3	3	26	62	0	54	42	6	5.5	12.0	72	42.7%	.296

Comparables: Mychal Givens, Jeurys Familia, Kelvin Herrera

Rosenthal is a great example of reliever variance. It would've been justifiable to think his big-league career was nearing its end after he allowed seven runs and recorded zero outs over his first four appearances in 2019. Instead, Rosenthal reestablished himself in 2020. Following a deadline deal that sent him out west, he permitted just one run and one walk while fanning 17 of the 35 batters he faced. Rosenthal did throw an uneasy amount of pitches down the middle, but he got away with it more often than not. Much like the failson of an oil tycoon, he should keep getting jobs so long as he can pump gas and avoid fires.

YEAR	TEAM	LVL	AGE	WHIP	ERA	DRA-	WARP	MPH	FB%	WHF	CSP
2019	HBG	AA	29	1.71	5.79	124	-0.2				
2019	TOL	AAA	29	2.62	10.12	163	-0.1				
2019	WAS	MLB	29	3.63	22.74	155	-0.2	99.9	75.5%	25.7%	
2019	DET	MLB	29	1.56	7.00	125	-0.1	99.8	68.8%	33.3%	
2020	SD	MLB	30	0.85	1.90	61	0.7	100.0	71.1%	37.7%	
2021 FS	SD	MLB	31	1.41	4.04	92	0.5	99.9	71.5%	34.3%	46.0%
2021 DC	SD	MLB	31	1.41	4.04	92	0.5	99.9	71.5%	34.3%	46.0%

Trevor Rosenthal, continued

Pitch Shape vs LHH

Pitch Shape vs RHH

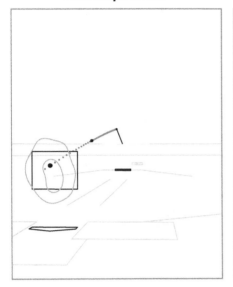
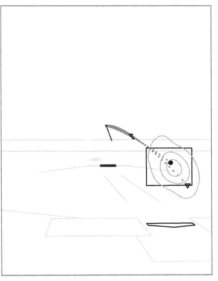

Type		Frequency	Velocity	H Movement	V Movement
●	Fastball	70.9%	98.1 [118]	-5.3 [107]	-9.5 [116]
▲	Changeup	8.4%	88 [111]	-11.6 [100]	-21.1 [118]
▽	Slider	20.5%	87.6 [116]	4.5 [97]	-31.9 [105]

Blake Snell LHP

Born: 12/04/92   Age: 28   Bats: L   Throws: L
Height: 6'4"   Weight: 225   Origin: Round 1, 2011 Draft (#52 overall)

YEAR	TEAM	LVL	AGE	W	L	SV	G	GS	IP	H	HR	BB/9	K/9	K	GB%	BABIP
2018	TB	MLB	25	21	5	0	31	31	180²	112	16	3.2	11.0	220	44.7%	.242
2019	TB	MLB	26	6	8	0	23	23	107	96	14	3.4	12.4	147	37.9%	.343
2020	TB	MLB	27	4	2	0	11	11	50	42	10	3.2	11.3	63	48.4%	.288
2021 FS	SD	MLB	28	10	7	0	26	26	150	118	16	3.9	11.6	193	43.8%	.289
2021 DC	SD	MLB	28	10	7	0	27	27	148.7	117	16	3.9	11.6	191	43.8%	.289

Comparables: Joe Musgrove, Nick Pivetta, Jakob Junis

You know the story by now, but, for posterity's sake: Snell was rolling in Game 6 of the World Series. He got into a little bit of trouble and Kevin Cash pulled him. It didn't work out—Nick Anderson continued his woeful October—and the Rays lost. Cash's decision to yank Snell has been debated to death—somehow, the likelihood that the Rays' plan works if they just insert one of their non-gassed relievers gets ignored—so we're not going to relegislate it here. What we will do is note that Snell popped up in trade rumors over the winter, and his eventual exit from Tampa Bay will go a long way in answering whether he's fancier Ryan Yarbrough or a legitimate front-of-the-rotation stud who should be left in during the most important game of the—wait, here comes Cash to make an author change. The Rays gave Snell another quick hook over the winter, moving him to the Padres despite three years of team control remaining on his below-market deal.

YEAR	TEAM	LVL	AGE	WHIP	ERA	DRA-	WARP	MPH	FB%	WHF	CSP
2018	TB	MLB	25	0.97	1.89	54	6.0	97.8	51.4%	34.7%	
2019	TB	MLB	26	1.27	4.29	73	2.5	97.2	48.4%	38.2%	
2020	TB	MLB	27	1.20	3.24	82	0.9	96.8	50.6%	34.0%	
2021 FS	SD	MLB	28	1.22	3.06	74	3.6	97.3	49.9%	35.9%	43.0%
2021 DC	SD	MLB	28	1.22	3.06	74	3.6	97.3	49.9%	35.9%	43.0%

Blake Snell, continued

Pitch Shape vs LHH

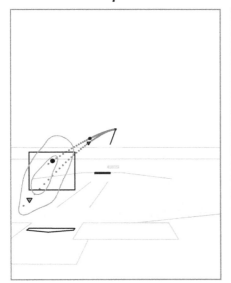

Pitch Shape vs RHH

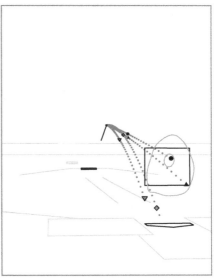

Type		Frequency	Velocity	H Movement	V Movement
●	Fastball	50.6%	95.3 [109]	5.1 [108]	-10.9 [112]
▲	Changeup	19.8%	88.2 [112]	11.5 [101]	-21.7 [116]
▽	Slider	15.0%	87.6 [117]	-3.3 [93]	-29.1 [113]
◇	Curveball	14.6%	80.4 [107]	-8.5 [104]	-47.5 [102]

Craig Stammen RHP

Born: 03/09/84   Age: 37   Bats: R   Throws: R
Height: 6'2"   Weight: 228   Origin: Round 12, 2005 Draft (#354 overall)

YEAR	TEAM	LVL	AGE	W	L	SV	G	GS	IP	H	HR	BB/9	K/9	K	GB%	BABIP
2018	SD	MLB	34	8	3	0	73	0	79	65	3	1.9	10.0	88	48.8%	.304
2019	SD	MLB	35	8	7	4	76	0	82	80	13	1.6	8.0	73	50.6%	.284
2020	SD	MLB	36	4	2	0	24	0	24	27	2	1.5	7.5	20	57.0%	.333
2021 FS	SD	MLB	37	2	2	0	57	0	50	47	5	2.1	8.0	44	52.9%	.289
2021 DC	SD	MLB	37	2	2	0	50	0	41	39	4	2.1	8.0	36	52.9%	.289

Comparables: Jesse Chavez, Matt Belisle, Mark Guthrie

A lot of care needs to be exercised in drawing conclusions from the pandemic-shortened season, and Stammen is a prime example of that. If you only look at his runs allowed, it seems as if he had a brutal year.Au contraire! Stammen actually improved his DRA from year-to-year by making gains with his strikeout, walk and home-run rates. He gave up a few more hits, but otherwise appeared to be just as good (or perhaps better) than he was the year before.

YEAR	TEAM	LVL	AGE	WHIP	ERA	DRA-	WARP	MPH	FB%	WHF	CSP
2018	SD	MLB	34	1.04	2.73	63	1.9	93.5	67.6%	29.8%	
2019	SD	MLB	35	1.16	3.29	87	1.0	94.5	72.2%	21.6%	
2020	SD	MLB	36	1.29	5.62	78	0.5	93.8	82.5%	24.1%	
2021 FS	SD	MLB	37	1.19	3.34	83	0.7	94.1	73.6%	24.1%	46.9%
2021 DC	SD	MLB	37	1.19	3.34	83	0.6	94.1	73.6%	24.1%	46.9%

Craig Stammen, continued

Pitch Shape vs LHH

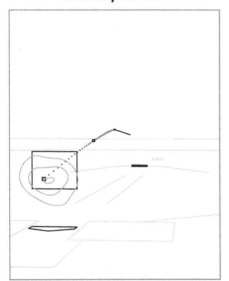

Pitch Shape vs RHH

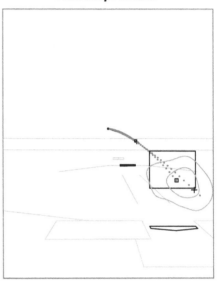

Type	Frequency	Velocity	H Movement	V Movement
● Fastball	3.4%	92.4 [100]	-9.6 [86]	-14.4 [102]
□ Sinker	62.1%	92.1 [98]	-11.9 [108]	-19 [105]
+ Cutter	17.0%	88.9 [104]	1 [94]	-24.2 [100]
▽ Slider	4.2%	85.7 [108]	0.7 [83]	-30.2 [110]
◇ Curveball	12.2%	80.6 [108]	7.1 [98]	-48.1 [101]

Matt Strahm LHP

Born: 11/12/91   Age: 29   Bats: R   Throws: L
Height: 6'2"   Weight: 190   Origin: Round 21, 2012 Draft (#643 overall)

YEAR	TEAM	LVL	AGE	W	L	SV	G	GS	IP	H	HR	BB/9	K/9	K	GB%	BABIP
2018	SA	AA	26	1	0	0	9	2	14¹	14	1	2.5	13.8	22	42.4%	.406
2018	SD	MLB	26	3	4	0	41	5	61¹	39	6	3.1	10.1	69	35.5%	.228
2019	SD	MLB	27	6	11	0	46	16	114²	121	22	1.7	9.3	118	35.6%	.315
2020	SD	MLB	28	0	1	0	19	0	20²	14	3	1.7	6.5	15	44.1%	.196
2021 FS	SD	MLB	29	2	2	0	57	0	50	45	7	2.5	9.1	50	38.8%	.284
2021 DC	SD	MLB	29	2	2	0	50	0	47	43	7	2.5	9.1	47	38.8%	.284

Comparables: Michael Lorenzen, Carlos Martínez, Austin Brice

Clevinger's long lost left-handed brother was used exclusively out of the bullpen for the first time in his career, and not solely against lefties, either. Considering Strahm's starter/reliever splits, it's probably the best route for him going forward. He has done a tremendous job at limiting walks, especially compared to the beginning of his career, when he'd hand out free passes every other inning. That growth has made it easier to buy into him as a solid enough middle-relief option for now and for years to come. Strahm required knee surgery after the season, though he is expected to be ready for game action by the time you flip this page.

YEAR	TEAM	LVL	AGE	WHIP	ERA	DRA-	WARP	MPH	FB%	WHF	CSP
2018	SA	AA	26	1.26	2.51	71	0.3				
2018	SD	MLB	26	0.98	2.05	88	0.7	95.5	58.0%	27.9%	
2019	SD	MLB	27	1.25	4.71	88	1.7	94.0	38.1%	23.5%	
2020	SD	MLB	28	0.87	2.61	100	0.2	94.3	55.8%	22.1%	
2021 FS	SD	MLB	29	1.19	3.74	90	0.5	94.3	44.8%	24.1%	53.6%
2021 DC	SD	MLB	29	1.19	3.74	90	0.5	94.3	44.8%	24.1%	53.6%

Matt Strahm, continued

Pitch Shape vs LHH

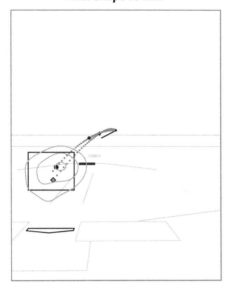

Pitch Shape vs RHH

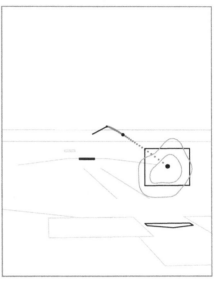

Type	Frequency	Velocity	H Movement	V Movement
● Fastball	55.8%	93 [101]	14.6 [62]	-19 [89]
▲ Changeup	10.4%	85.9 [103]	16.2 [76]	-29.9 [93]
▽ Slider	14.0%	85.9 [109]	-2.3 [89]	-26.6 [121]
◇ Curveball	19.8%	81.4 [111]	-6.2 [94]	-37.8 [124]

Taylor Williams   RHP

Born: 07/21/91   Age: 29   Bats: S   Throws: R
Height: 5'11"   Weight: 185   Origin: Round 4, 2013 Draft (#122 overall)

YEAR	TEAM	LVL	AGE	W	L	SV	G	GS	IP	H	HR	BB/9	K/9	K	GB%	BABIP
2018	MIL	MLB	26	1	3	0	56	0	53	53	6	4.2	9.7	57	35.9%	.329
2019	SA	AAA	27	3	3	6	46	0	54	40	8	3.5	9.5	57	53.1%	.242
2019	MIL	MLB	27	1	1	0	10	0	14²	22	1	4.3	9.2	15	59.2%	.438
2020	SD	MLB	28	1	1	6	15	0	14²	14	1	4.3	12.3	20	40.5%	.361
2021 FS	SD	MLB	29	2	2	0	57	0	50	45	6	4.1	9.9	55	45.6%	.295
2021 DC	SD	MLB	29	0	0	0	16	0	17.7	16	2	4.1	9.9	19	45.6%	.295

Comparables: Dominic Leone, Cam Bedrosian, Shawn Armstrong

Williams landed in San Diego at the 2020 trade deadline, but he made only one appearance after the deal, an outing in which he faced five batters and gave up a run. His underlying measures suggest he's much better than his unsightly career run average.

YEAR	TEAM	LVL	AGE	WHIP	ERA	DRA-	WARP	MPH	FB%	WHF	CSP
2018	MIL	MLB	26	1.47	4.25	96	0.4	97.1	64.9%	32.5%	
2019	SA	AAA	27	1.13	2.83	53	1.9				
2019	MIL	MLB	27	1.98	9.82	101	0.1	96.7	63.3%	26.4%	
2020	SD	MLB	28	1.43	6.14	81	0.3	96.2	45.2%	31.9%	
2021 FS	SD	MLB	29	1.36	4.15	96	0.4	96.7	57.5%	30.8%	44.2%
2021 DC	SD	MLB	29	1.36	4.15	96	0.1	96.7	57.5%	30.8%	44.2%

Taylor Williams, continued

Pitch Shape vs LHH

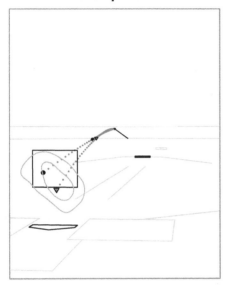

Pitch Shape vs RHH

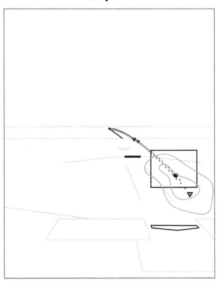

Type	Frequency	Velocity	H Movement	V Movement
● Fastball	43.8%	95.2 [108]	-10.4 [82]	-17.6 [93]
▽ Slider	54.0%	86 [109]	0.5 [82]	-31.8 [106]

PLAYER COMMENTS WITHOUT GRAPHS

CJ Abrams SS
Born: 10/03/00   Age: 20   Bats: L   Throws: R
Height: 6'2"   Weight: 185   Origin: Round 1, 2019 Draft (#6 overall)

YEAR	TEAM	LVL	AGE	PA	R	2B	3B	HR	RBI	BB	K	SB	CS	AVG/OBP/SLG
2019	SD1	ROK	18	156	40	12	8	3	22	10	14	14	6	.401/.442/.662
2019	FW	LO-A	18	9	1	1	0	0	0	1	0	1	0	.250/.333/.375
2021 FS	SD	MLB	20	600	49	24	5	7	53	31	133	27	9	.235/.281/.342

Comparables: Yu Chang, Christian Arroyo, Tyrone Taylor

Abrams, the sixth pick in the 2019 draft, is one of the top shortstop prospects in baseball thanks to his above-average power-speed potential. If there's one thing the Padres need, it's another dynamic young shortstop.

YEAR	TEAM	LVL	AGE	PA	DRC+	BABIP	BRR	FRAA	WARP
2019	SD1	ROK	18	156		.425			
2019	FW	LO-A	18	9	121	.250	0.1	SS(1): -0.1	0.0
2021 FS	SD	MLB	20	600	71	.295	3.0	SS 5	0.5

Luis Campusano C
Born: 09/29/98   Age: 22   Bats: R   Throws: R
Height: 5'11"   Weight: 232   Origin: Round 2, 2017 Draft (#39 overall)

YEAR	TEAM	LVL	AGE	PA	R	2B	3B	HR	RBI	BB	K	SB	CS	AVG/OBP/SLG
2018	FW	LO-A	19	284	26	11	0	3	40	19	43	0	1	.288/.345/.365
2019	LE	HI-A	20	482	63	31	1	15	80	52	57	0	0	.321/.394/.508
2020	SD	MLB	21	4	2	0	0	1	1	0	2	0	0	.333/.500/1.333
2021 FS	SD	MLB	22	600	74	28	1	17	74	41	138	0	1	.256/.311/.408
2021 DC	SD	MLB	22	125	15	6	0	3	15	8	28	0	0	.256/.311/.408

Comparables: Alejandro Kirk, Jarrod Saltalamacchia, Chance Sisco

In the span of two months, Campusano experienced the high of hitting a home run in his big-league debut, and the low of being arrested in Georgia for felony marijuana possession. Per the *San Diego Union-Tribune*, Campusano had 79 grams of weed in his possession when he was pulled over. State law stipulates that having more than 28.35 grams (or an ounce) is a felony that is punishable by up to 10 years in jail. If Campusano's arrest is a blemish on anything, it's on a society that stomachs such harsh penalties for harmless acts.

YEAR	TEAM	LVL	AGE	PA	DRC+	BABIP	BRR	FRAA	WARP
2018	FW	LO-A	19	284	116	.335	-1.1	C(38): -0.8, 1B(4): 0.2	0.8
2019	LE	HI-A	20	482	167	.336	-4.4	C(76): -2.6, 1B(2): 0.0	3.9
2020	SD	MLB	21	4	81				0.0
2021 FS	SD	MLB	22	600	98	.309	-1.0	C 0, 1B 0	2.1
2021 DC	SD	MLB	22	125	98	.309	-0.2	C 0	0.5

Robert Hassell III   CF

Born: 08/15/01   Age: 19   Bats: L   Throws: L
Height: 6'2"   Weight: 195   Origin: Round 1, 2020 Draft (#8 overall)

Leading up to the draft, there were persistent rumors that the Padres just absolutely loved Hassell and his beautiful swing. They panned out when the team popped him a pick ahead of Zac Veen, a more touted prep outfielder, and quickly signed him away from his Vanderbilt commitment to bring him to the alternate site. As befitting the aesthetic adjectives attached by all to his smooth left-handed stroke, Hassell has an extremely advanced hit tool for a high school bat, along with projectable power for down the road. He was a legitimate prospect on the mound as well, enough so that there were ideas that he might be a two-way player as a pro, though the Padres aren't planning on using him as such. If he can achieve success in pro ball, he'll be one of the best outfield prospects around—maybe even one of the best prospects, period—in short order.

Hudson Head   CF

Born: 04/08/01   Age: 20   Bats: L   Throws: L
Height: 6'1"   Weight: 180   Origin: Round 3, 2019 Draft (#84 overall)

YEAR	TEAM	LVL	AGE	PA	R	2B	3B	HR	RBI	BB	K	SB	CS	AVG/OBP/SLG
2019	SD1	ROK	18	141	19	7	3	1	12	15	29	3	3	.283/.383/.417
2021 FS	SD	MLB	20	600	44	18	3	8	47	34	203	5	4	.189/.243/.278

Comparables: Byron Buxton, Ronald Acuña Jr., Aaron Hicks

Head, a center-field quality athlete with a promising stick, has a chance to be the third big-league player to hail from Winston Churchill High School in Texas, joining Scott Dunn and Randy Choate.

YEAR	TEAM	LVL	AGE	PA	DRC+	BABIP	BRR	FRAA	WARP
2019	SD1	ROK	18	141		.363			
2021 FS	SD	MLB	20	600	43	.279	0.5	CF -10	-3.5

Ha-seong Kim   SS

Born: 10/17/95   Age: 25   Bats: R   Throws: R
Height: 5'9"   Weight: 168   Origin: International Free Agent, 2020

YEAR	TEAM	LVL	AGE	PA	R	2B	3B	HR	RBI	BB	K	SB	CS	AVG/OBP/SLG
2021 FS	SD	MLB	25	600	65	23	2	10	64	41	108			.238/.295/.346
2021 DC	SD	MLB	25	499	54	19	1	8	53	34	90			.238/.295/.346

Late in the season, Kiwoom announced that they would be posting their shortstop over the winter, allowing Kim to pursue a lifelong dream of playing in the major leagues. While there's some debate over how well, and how quickly, Kim's promising bat will acclimate to MLB arms, there's little doubt that he's the best hitter to ever arrive from the KBO. Easily a top-100 prospect in baseball, the 25-year-old Kim was the best athlete in the KBO last year and he's pretty clearly outgrown his native league. Offensively, he's a complete player, demonstrating his abilities to make contact, hit with power, gauge the strike zone and even steal bases. Defensively, reviews are mixed. He's a plus runner with a good first step, and he has more than enough range to play short in the big leagues. His arm is good enough as well, though not plus, and given his accuracy issues (particularly on the run) it's fair to round down and grade it as average. While he gets to plenty of balls, his hands aren't the cleanest, and when you add it all up, there's a chance that he ultimately fits better at second or third. Regardless, Kim should be at least a good regular, and if his bat translates he could be the biggest transpacific sensation since Ichiro.

YEAR	TEAM	LVL	AGE	PA	DRC+	BABIP	BRR	FRAA	WARP
2021 FS	SD	MLB	25	600	79	.276			0.1
2021 DC	SD	MLB	25	499	79	.276		2B 0	0.1

Jorge Mateo   SS

Born: 06/23/95   Age: 26   Bats: R   Throws: R
Height: 6'0"   Weight: 182   Origin: International Free Agent, 2012

YEAR	TEAM	LVL	AGE	PA	R	2B	3B	HR	RBI	BB	K	SB	CS	AVG/OBP/SLG
2018	NAS	AAA	23	510	50	17	16	3	45	29	139	25	10	.230/.280/.353
2019	LV	AAA	24	566	95	29	14	19	78	29	145	24	11	.289/.330/.504
2020	SD	MLB	25	28	4	3	0	0	2	1	11	1	0	.154/.185/.269
2021 FS	SD	MLB	26	600	66	24	6	15	65	34	193	19	8	.217/.265/.367
2021 DC	SD	MLB	26	153	17	6	1	3	16	8	49	4	2	.217/.265/.367

Comparables: Erick Mejia, Robert Andino, Jonathan Villar

It's fair to write that Mateo's only real skill is running fast. It's also fair to write that we're as surprised as you are that his comment doesn't appear in the Royals chapter.

YEAR	TEAM	LVL	AGE	PA	DRC+	BABIP	BRR	FRAA	WARP
2018	NAS	AAA	23	510	57	.316	1.1	SS(123): -0.8, 2B(4): -0.5	-0.8
2019	LV	AAA	24	566	81	.366	3.2	SS(100): 16.6, 2B(14): -0.2	2.9
2020	SD	MLB	25	28	66	.267	-0.7	2B(5): 0.6, LF(3): -0.0, RF(3): -0.1	-0.1
2021 FS	*SD*	*MLB*	*26*	*600*	*71*	*.299*	*2.7*	*CF 0, 2B 1*	*0.0*
2021 DC	*SD*	*MLB*	*26*	*153*	*71*	*.299*	*0.7*	*3B 0, CF 0*	*-0.1*

Brian O'Grady OF

Born: 05/17/92   Age: 29   Bats: L   Throws: R
Height: 6'2"   Weight: 215   Origin: Round 8, 2014 Draft (#245 overall)

YEAR	TEAM	LVL	AGE	PA	R	2B	3B	HR	RBI	BB	K	SB	CS	AVG/OBP/SLG
2018	PNS	AA	26	214	27	12	4	6	30	27	41	4	1	.258/.354/.472
2018	LOU	AAA	26	162	27	9	2	8	29	12	39	5	4	.306/.365/.562
2019	LOU	AAA	27	489	71	30	1	28	77	51	136	20	4	.280/.359/.550
2019	CIN	MLB	27	48	4	2	1	2	3	4	17	0	0	.190/.292/.429
2020	TB	MLB	28	5	2	1	0	0	0	0	1	1	0	.400/.400/.600
2021 FS	*SD*	*MLB*	*29*	*600*	*71*	*25*	*4*	*20*	*71*	*58*	*190*	*5*	*3*	*.213/.299/.393*
2021 DC	*SD*	*MLB*	*29*	*128*	*15*	*5*	*0*	*4*	*15*	*12*	*40*	*0*	*1*	*.213/.299/.393*

Comparables: Mitch Jones, Travis Ishikawa, Matt Clark

O'Grady saw action at three positions in two games last season with the Rays. His three-corners versatility and left-handed pop (he homered 30 times in 2019) should enable him to have some kind of big-league career as a bench player. The more important matter, if you ask us, is whether he'll be christened as the Notorious B.O.G. or Beef O'Grady. Can't go wrong either way, we s'pose.

YEAR	TEAM	LVL	AGE	PA	DRC+	BABIP	BRR	FRAA	WARP
2018	PNS	AA	26	214	123	.294	-1.5	LF(23): -2.8, 1B(12): -0.1, RF(12): 0.5	0.1
2018	LOU	AAA	26	162	135	.367	0.4	LF(29): -0.6, 1B(12): 0.6, CF(2): 0.0	0.8
2019	LOU	AAA	27	489	111	.342	2.0	1B(64): -1.5, CF(33): 1.6, LF(15): 1.6	1.8
2019	CIN	MLB	27	48	75	.261	-0.5	CF(11): -0.2, LF(6): 0.1, 1B(2): -0.2	-0.1
2020	TB	MLB	28	5	83	.500	0.2	1B(1): -0.0, LF(1): -0.0, CF(1): -0.1	0.0
2021 FS	*SD*	*MLB*	*29*	*600*	*87*	*.289*	*0.2*	*CF 3, RF -1*	*0.6*
2021 DC	*SD*	*MLB*	*29*	*128*	*87*	*.289*	*0.1*	*CF 1, RF 0*	*0.2*

Jorge Oña   OF

Born: 12/31/96   Age: 24   Bats: R   Throws: R
Height: 6'0"   Weight: 235   Origin: International Free Agent, 2016

YEAR	TEAM	LVL	AGE	PA	R	2B	3B	HR	RBI	BB	K	SB	CS	AVG/OBP/SLG
2018	LE	HI-A	21	410	44	24	2	8	44	33	110	0	2	.239/.312/.380
2019	AMA	AA	22	103	11	2	0	5	18	11	26	2	1	.348/.417/.539
2020	SD	MLB	23	15	3	1	0	1	2	2	7	0	0	.250/.400/.583
2021 FS	SD	MLB	24	600	71	17	1	18	67	49	211	0	1	.209/.282/.349
2021 DC	SD	MLB	24	93	11	2	0	2	10	7	32	0	0	.209/.282/.349

Comparables: Rymer Liriano, Zoilo Almonte, Marcell Ozuna

Oña's strikeout and fielding woes have always been concerning, but the universal DH could well give him a chance at a career that entails more than being a designated pinch-hitter—well, sort of, anyway.

YEAR	TEAM	LVL	AGE	PA	DRC+	BABIP	BRR	FRAA	WARP
2018	LE	HI-A	21	410	88	.317	-2.1	RF(59): -1.3	-1.3
2019	AMA	AA	22	103	170	.433	0.7	LF(15): -2.3	0.6
2020	SD	MLB	23	15	78	.500	0.1	RF(1): -0.0	0.0
2021 FS	SD	MLB	24	600	75	.301	-0.7	RF 2, LF 0	-0.5
2021 DC	SD	MLB	24	93	75	.301	-0.1	RF 0	-0.1

Jamie Romak   RF

Born: 09/30/85   Age: 35   Bats: R   Throws: R
Height: 6'2"   Weight: 220   Origin: Round 4, 2003 Draft (#127 overall)

YEAR	TEAM	LVL	AGE	PA	R	2B	3B	HR	RBI	BB	K	SB	CS	AVG/OBP/SLG
2018	SK	KBO	32	616	102	19	0	43	107	72	123	10	5	.316/.404/.597
2019	SK	KBO	33	589	86	28	1	29	95	73	117	6	3	.276/.370/.508
2020	SK	KBO	34	586	85	32	0	32	91	91	116	4	2	.282/.399/.546
2021								No projection						

As SK slogged through a dreadful and disappointing season, Romak managed to endure the campaign without once changing facial expressions. Perhaps that natural stoicism goes some way toward explaining his extremely consistent production since joining the Wyverns back in 2017. Thirty-five years old now, Romak is too old to get another big league shot, but young enough to post a few more 130 OPS+ seasons in Korea before he hangs 'em up.

YEAR	TEAM	LVL	AGE	PA	DRC+	BABIP	BRR	FRAA	WARP
2018	SK	KBO	32	616					
2019	SK	KBO	33	589					
2020	SK	KBO	34	586					
2021					No projection				

Austin Adams   RHP

Born: 05/05/91   Age: 30   Bats: R   Throws: R
Height: 6'3"   Weight: 220   Origin: Round 8, 2012 Draft (#267 overall)

YEAR	TEAM	LVL	AGE	W	L	SV	G	GS	IP	H	HR	BB/9	K/9	K	GB%	BABIP
2018	SYR	AAA	27	1	4	9	41	0	46¹	47	1	3.9	15.2	78	40.2%	.447
2018	WAS	MLB	27	0	0	0	2	0	1	1	0	27.0	0.0	0	50.0%	.250
2019	FRE	AAA	28	0	1	1	8	0	10	7	0	2.7	18.0	20	47.1%	.412
2019	SEA	MLB	28	2	2	0	29	2	31	20	4	4.1	14.8	51	49.2%	.291
2019	WAS	MLB	28	0	0	0	1	0	1	0	0	18.0	18.0	2	100.0%	.000
2020	SD	MLB	29	0	0	0	3	0	4	3	1	4.5	15.8	7	50.0%	.286
2021 FS	SD	MLB	30	2	2	0	57	0	50	37	5	5.5	14.1	78	44.5%	.311
2021 DC	SD	MLB	30	1	1	0	33	0	47	35	5	5.5	14.1	73	44.5%	.311

Comparables: Shawn Armstrong, Richard Rodríguez, Emilio Pagán

Adams didn't make his season debut until late in the season because of a torn ACL suffered in 2019. When he took the mound, he was more reliant on his wipeout slider than ever, throwing it nearly 90 percent of the time. His high walk rate will make Padres fans and coaches nervous, but his excellent ability to miss bats should help limit the damage.

YEAR	TEAM	LVL	AGE	WHIP	ERA	DRA-	WARP	MPH	FB%	WHF	CSP
2018	SYR	AAA	27	1.45	3.50	28	1.9				
2018	WAS	MLB	27	4.00	0.00	223	-0.1	96.2	58.3%	20.0%	
2019	FRE	AAA	28	1.00	2.70	33	0.4				
2019	SEA	MLB	28	1.10	3.77	54	0.9	96.6	35.2%	41.1%	
2019	WAS	MLB	28	2.00	9.00	50	0.0	95.7	51.5%	22.2%	
2020	SD	MLB	29	1.25	4.50	85	0.1	94.6	16.2%	48.0%	
2021 FS	SD	MLB	30	1.36	3.71	85	0.7	96.2	33.2%	41.3%	44.3%
2021 DC	SD	MLB	30	1.36	3.71	85	0.6	96.2	33.2%	41.3%	44.3%

Michel Baez RHP

Born: 01/21/96   Age: 25   Bats: R   Throws: R
Height: 6'8"   Weight: 220   Origin: International Free Agent, 2016

YEAR	TEAM	LVL	AGE	W	L	SV	G	GS	IP	H	HR	BB/9	K/9	K	GB%	BABIP
2018	LE	HI-A	22	4	7	0	17	17	86²	73	5	3.4	9.6	92	34.6%	.304
2018	SA	AA	22	0	3	0	4	4	18¹	22	4	5.9	10.3	21	30.8%	.375
2019	AMA	AA	23	3	2	1	15	0	27	22	1	3.7	12.7	38	37.5%	.333
2019	SD	MLB	23	1	1	0	24	1	29²	25	3	4.2	8.5	28	38.4%	.268
2020	SD	MLB	24	0	0	0	3	1	4²	7	0	3.9	13.5	7	35.7%	.500
2021 FS	SD	MLB	25	2	2	0	57	0	50	45	8	4.0	9.7	53	36.6%	.286
2021 DC	SD	MLB	25	2	2	0	25	3	24.7	22	4	4.0	9.7	26	36.6%	.286

Comparables: Ryan Perry, Miguel Castro, Kevin Siegrist

Báez hasn't thrown at least six innings in an appearance since August 2018. He's spent the past two years pitching almost exclusively out of the bullpens. His arsenal includes two good pitches in his mid-90s fastball and changeup, as well as a few other below-average offerings. Any which way you slice it, Báez is probably a reliever.Given the opportunity, he could be a pretty good one.

YEAR	TEAM	LVL	AGE	WHIP	ERA	DRA-	WARP	MPH	FB%	WHF	CSP
2018	LE	HI-A	22	1.22	2.91	79	1.4				
2018	SA	AA	22	1.85	7.36	65	0.4				
2019	AMA	AA	23	1.22	2.00	70	0.4				
2019	SD	MLB	23	1.31	3.03	117	-0.1	97.4	58.7%	24.0%	
2020	SD	MLB	24	1.93	7.71	81	0.1	96.4	55.6%	26.1%	
2021 FS	SD	MLB	25	1.34	4.33	100	0.2	97.2	58.0%	24.5%	41.1%
2021 DC	SD	MLB	25	1.34	4.33	100	0.2	97.2	58.0%	24.5%	41.1%

Nick Burdi   RHP

Born: 01/19/93   Age: 28   Bats: R   Throws: R
Height: 6'3"   Weight: 225   Origin: Round 2, 2014 Draft (#46 overall)

YEAR	TEAM	LVL	AGE	W	L	SV	G	GS	IP	H	HR	BB/9	K/9	K	GB%	BABIP
2018	IND	AAA	25	0	2	0	5	0	5	9	0	7.2	9.0	5	31.6%	.474
2018	PIT	MLB	25	0	0	0	2	0	1¹	3	1	13.5	13.5	2	33.3%	.400
2019	PIT	MLB	26	2	1	0	11	0	8²	11	1	3.1	17.7	17	20.0%	.526
2020	PIT	MLB	27	0	1	1	3	0	2¹	2	0	7.7	15.4	4	25.0%	.500
2021 FS	SD	MLB	28	2	2	0	57	0	50	40	7	4.3	11.2	62	37.8%	.289

Comparables: Jimmie Sherfy, Rowan Wick, Sam Freeman

What ancient ill lies heavy over the house Burdi? Like brother Zack, Nick has struggled with injuries over his career, but seemed poised to open 2020 as the Pirates' closer, armed with his triple-digit fastball and wipeout slider. Instead he pitched all of 2.1 innings before going on the IL, and wound up having a second Tommy John surgery in October, with a lengthy timetable (16-18 months) to return. Pittsburgh designated Burdi in November, paving the way for the Padres to add him over the winter. Given that closers are worth millions and interns are cheap, it's probably still worth poking around in the woods outside Casa Burdi for a cursed amulet buried beneath a lightning-blasted tree, just in case.

YEAR	TEAM	LVL	AGE	WHIP	ERA	DRA-	WARP	MPH	FB%	WHF	CSP
2018	IND	AAA	25	2.60	5.40	64	0.1				
2018	PIT	MLB	25	3.75	20.25	40	0.0	98.5	71.4%	35.7%	
2019	PIT	MLB	26	1.62	9.35	54	0.3	98.2	45.3%	36.6%	
2020	PIT	MLB	27	1.71	3.86	97	0.0	99.6	54.3%	35.0%	
2021 FS	SD	MLB	28	1.29	3.85	87	0.6	98.6	49.7%	36.1%	48.5%

José Castillo   LHP

Born: 01/10/96   Age: 25   Bats: L   Throws: L
Height: 6'6"   Weight: 252   Origin: International Free Agent, 2012

YEAR	TEAM	LVL	AGE	W	L	SV	G	GS	IP	H	HR	BB/9	K/9	K	GB%	BABIP
2018	SA	AA	22	2	1	5	12	0	15	14	0	4.8	15.6	26	34.4%	.452
2018	ELP	AAA	22	1	0	3	10	0	11¹	6	1	1.6	10.3	13	39.3%	.192
2018	SD	MLB	22	3	3	0	37	0	38¹	23	3	2.8	12.2	52	37.3%	.250
2019	SD	MLB	23	0	0	0	1	0	0²	0	0	13.5	27.0	2		
2021 FS	SD	MLB	25	2	2	0	57	0	50	42	7	4.6	11.5	63	37.2%	.295
2021 DC	SD	MLB	25	1	1	0	33	0	23.3	19	3	4.6	11.5	30	37.2%	.295

Comparables: Mauricio Cabrera, Cionel Pérez, Jacob Nix

Castillo missed all of 2020 because of shoulder trouble, bringing his two-year total to 10 appearances between the majors and the minors. He turned 25 in January, so he still has time to get healthy and have a legitimate career as a setup pitcher.

YEAR	TEAM	LVL	AGE	WHIP	ERA	DRA-	WARP	MPH	FB%	WHF	CSP
2018	SA	AA	22	1.47	3.00	44	0.5				
2018	ELP	AAA	22	0.71	0.79	70	0.2				
2018	SD	MLB	22	0.91	3.29	67	0.8	97.0	55.2%	33.9%	
2019	SD	MLB	23	1.50	0.00	106	0.0	96.7	64.7%	40.0%	
2021 FS	SD	MLB	25	1.35	4.06	94	0.4	97.0	55.7%	34.2%	48.2%
2021 DC	SD	MLB	25	1.35	4.06	94	0.2	97.0	55.7%	34.2%	48.2%

Nabil Crismatt   RHP

Born: 12/25/94   Age: 26   Bats: R   Throws: R
Height: 6'1"   Weight: 220   Origin: International Free Agent, 2011

YEAR	TEAM	LVL	AGE	W	L	SV	G	GS	IP	H	HR	BB/9	K/9	K	GB%	BABIP
2018	BNG	AA	23	8	6	0	18	18	105¹	95	8	3.2	9.0	105	44.6%	.309
2018	LV	AAA	23	3	4	0	9	9	38²	61	8	4.4	8.1	35	44.6%	.421
2019	ARK	AA	24	4	5	0	14	13	83²	57	6	1.2	9.6	89	43.3%	.242
2019	TAC	AAA	24	0	5	0	13	8	46²	67	15	4.0	13.1	68	33.8%	.419
2020	STL	MLB	25	0	0	0	6	0	8¹	6	2	1.1	8.6	8	50.0%	.200
2021 FS	SD	MLB	26	2	2	0	57	0	50	46	7	3.3	9.2	51	41.4%	.287
2021 DC	SD	MLB	26	2	2	0	25	3	24.7	22	3	3.3	9.2	25	41.4%	.287

Comparables: Chase De Jong, Ryan Helsley, Andrew Moore

A few up-and-down innings in St. Louis last year did little to tell us whether Crismatt can make his low-velo mix work in a big-league bullpen, nor whether it's appropriate to call the pitch you most frequently throw a "changeup." Maybe Crismatt can provide more answers now that he's part of the Padres.

YEAR	TEAM	LVL	AGE	WHIP	ERA	DRA-	WARP	MPH	FB%	WHF	CSP
2018	BNG	AA	23	1.25	3.59	78	2.0				
2018	LV	AAA	23	2.07	8.84	99	0.4				
2019	ARK	AA	24	0.81	1.94	55	2.3				
2019	TAC	AAA	24	1.89	9.06	150	-0.3				
2020	STL	MLB	25	0.84	3.24	93	0.1	90.7	41.2%	27.4%	
2021 FS	SD	MLB	26	1.29	4.06	96	0.3	90.7	41.2%	27.4%	46.2%
2021 DC	SD	MLB	26	1.29	4.06	96	0.2	90.7	41.2%	27.4%	46.2%

MacKenzie Gore   LHP

Born: 02/24/99   Age: 22   Bats: L   Throws: L
Height: 6'2"   Weight: 197   Origin: Round 1, 2017 Draft (#3 overall)

YEAR	TEAM	LVL	AGE	W	L	SV	G	GS	IP	H	HR	BB/9	K/9	K	GB%	BABIP
2018	FW	LO-A	19	2	5	0	16	16	60²	61	5	2.7	11.0	74	40.5%	.354
2019	LE	HI-A	20	7	1	0	15	15	79¹	36	4	2.3	12.5	110	36.5%	.212
2019	AMA	AA	20	2	1	0	5	5	21²	20	3	3.3	10.4	25	44.6%	.321
2021 FS	SD	MLB	22	9	8	0	26	26	150	126	22	4.0	10.3	172	39.8%	.279
2021 DC	SD	MLB	22	3	3	0	12	11	56.7	47	8	4.0	10.3	65	39.8%	.279

Comparables: Brailyn Marquez, Deivi García, José Suarez

The shortened season and lack of a minor-league campaign robbed everyone of the debut of one of the game's best young pitchers. He's drawn Clayton Kershaw comparisons in the past because of his left-handedness, his fierce breaking ball and a high leg kick. Gore is unlikely to become Kershaw, mind you, but the upside is such that you can understand why the Padres resisted rushing him to the Show. If he ends up making his major league debut in 2021—and he ought to—he'll still be only 22 years old. What was once a weak Padres' rotation is coming along, but a fully realized Gore, meaning the version of him that can safely be described as a no. 2 starter, would go a long way towards helping San Diego stand toe-to-toe (and arm-to-arm) with the actual Kershaw, his Dodgers and the rest of the league's elite teams.

YEAR	TEAM	LVL	AGE	WHIP	ERA	DRA-	WARP	MPH	FB%	WHF	CSP
2018	FW	LO-A	19	1.30	4.45	59	1.8				
2019	LE	HI-A	20	0.71	1.02	34	3.2				
2019	AMA	AA	20	1.29	4.15	86	0.2				
2021 FS	SD	MLB	22	1.29	3.87	95	1.9				
2021 DC	SD	MLB	22	1.29	3.87	95	0.7				

Justin Lange   RHP

Born: 09/11/01   Age: 19   Bats: R   Throws: R
Height: 6'4"   Weight: 220   Origin: Round 1, 2020 Draft (#34 overall)

The Padres picked up hard-throwing Texas prep Lange with a competitive balance pick after the first round. After a major winter and spring velocity spike, he was suddenly sitting mid-90s and touching triple-digits leading up to the draft, making him one of the few late pop-ups in an amateur season that barely happened. Lange continued to impress at the alternate site and instructs, holding his gains and flashing a hard slider with significant promise. All caveats about high school pitchers aside—and Lange certainly does need a lot of work on command and secondary offerings—there's a lot of projection and hope here.

Nick Ramirez   LHP

Born: 08/01/89   Age: 31   Bats: L   Throws: L
Height: 6'4"   Weight: 232   Origin: Round 4, 2011 Draft (#131 overall)

YEAR	TEAM	LVL	AGE	W	L	SV	G	GS	IP	H	HR	BB/9	K/9	K	GB%	BABIP
2018	BLX	AA	28	8	0	1	19	0	30²	17	2	3.8	9.7	33	53.3%	.205
2018	RMV	AAA	28	3	3	0	20	2	37²	44	3	5.0	4.3	18	47.8%	.318
2019	ERI	AA	29	1	0	0	3	3	14¹	11	1	1.3	12.6	20	45.5%	.323
2019	TOL	AAA	29	0	1	0	2	2	9	12	1	3.0	10.0	10	44.8%	.393
2019	DET	MLB	29	5	4	0	46	0	79²	76	11	4.0	8.4	74	45.4%	.288
2020	DET	MLB	30	0	0	0	5	0	10²	8	3	3.4	9.3	11	50.0%	.185
2021 FS	SD	MLB	31	2	2	0	57	0	50	46	5	4.3	8.5	47	46.2%	.289

Comparables: Ryne Harper, Matt Grace, Brian Moran

It's always fun to go back and look at what players were when they were drafted: Jim Thome was a shortstop. Eddie Murray started off as a catcher. But conversions don't get more rare than Ramirez, who began as a first baseman before climbing onto the mound. A changeup artist by trade, he doesn't have the stamina to start or the velo to close, but he avoids hard contact consistently enough to labor multiple innings through during the soft, chewy, nougaty center of the game.

YEAR	TEAM	LVL	AGE	WHIP	ERA	DRA-	WARP	MPH	FB%	WHF	CSP
2018	BLX	AA	28	0.98	1.76	66	0.6				
2018	RMV	AAA	28	1.73	5.73	105	0.1				
2019	ERI	AA	29	0.91	2.51	61	0.3				
2019	TOL	AAA	29	1.67	2.00	106	0.1				
2019	DET	MLB	29	1.39	4.07	92	0.7	91.5	58.4%	28.2%	
2020	DET	MLB	30	1.12	5.91	102	0.1	91.3	60.8%	23.5%	
2021 FS	SD	MLB	31	1.41	4.25	98	0.3	91.5	58.8%	27.4%	41.3%

Ryan Weathers   LHP

Born: 12/17/99   Age: 21   Bats: R   Throws: L
Height: 6'1"   Weight: 230   Origin: Round 1, 2018 Draft (#7 overall)

YEAR	TEAM	LVL	AGE	W	L	SV	G	GS	IP	H	HR	BB/9	K/9	K	GB%	BABIP
2018	SD2	ROK	18	0	2	0	4	4	9^1	8	2	2.9	8.7	9	69.0%	.222
2018	FW	LO-A	18	0	1	0	3	3	9	11	0	1.0	9.0	9	54.8%	.367
2019	FW	LO-A	19	3	7	0	22	22	96	101	6	1.7	8.4	90	44.6%	.348
2021 FS	SD	MLB	21	2	3	0	57	0	50	48	7	3.3	7.1	39	43.2%	.275
2021 DC	SD	MLB	21	0	0	0	4	3	13.3	13	2	3.3	7.1	10	43.2%	.275

Comparables: Brailyn Marquez, Noah Syndergaard, Luis Severino

Weathers barely missed out on becoming the first pitcher to ever make his major-league debut during the playoffs, having been edged by Rays lefty Shane McClanahan. Though he pitched in relief, the way his father David used to, he's expected to have a career as a mid-to-back end starter thanks to a well-rounded arsenal and above-average command.

YEAR	TEAM	LVL	AGE	WHIP	ERA	DRA-	WARP	MPH	FB%	WHF	CSP
2018	SD2	ROK	18	1.18	3.86						
2018	FW	LO-A	18	1.33	3.00	82	0.1				
2019	FW	LO-A	19	1.24	3.84	112	-0.3				
2021 FS	SD	MLB	21	1.33	4.32	105	0.1				
2021 DC	SD	MLB	21	1.33	4.32	105	0.1				

Trey Wingenter   RHP

Born: 04/15/94   Age: 27   Bats: R   Throws: R
Height: 6'7"   Weight: 237   Origin: Round 17, 2015 Draft (#507 overall)

YEAR	TEAM	LVL	AGE	W	L	SV	G	GS	IP	H	HR	BB/9	K/9	K	GB%	BABIP
2018	ELP	AAA	24	3	3	4	40	0	44^1	29	4	4.9	10.8	53	48.1%	.250
2018	SD	MLB	24	0	0	0	22	0	19	13	3	5.2	12.8	27	40.5%	.256
2019	AMA	AA	25	0	1	0	1	0	0^2	2	1	13.5	13.5	1	33.3%	.500
2019	ELP	AAA	25	0	0	1	3	0	3^1	1	0	0.0	18.9	7	75.0%	.250
2019	SD	MLB	25	1	3	1	51	1	51	34	5	4.9	12.5	71	36.3%	.269
2021 FS	*SD*	*MLB*	*27*	*2*	*2*	*0*	*57*	*0*	*50*	*40*	*6*	*5.4*	*11.8*	*65*	*41.0%*	*.291*
2021 DC	*SD*	*MLB*	*27*	*0*	*0*	*0*	*11*	*0*	*11.7*	*9*	*1*	*5.4*	*11.8*	*15*	*41.0%*	*.291*

Comparables: Keynan Middleton, J.P. Feyereisen, Ian Gibaut

Wingenter's strikeout and whiff rates continue to be elite, but he's going to have trouble sticking around for long if his walk and strand rates remain elite as well, just not in the normal sense of the word. We feel safe suggesting better days are ahead—his hard-hit rate is in line with the league-average, suggesting there isn't some underlying contact-management flaw here—but we reserve the right to change our mind if he keeps having these problems through another season.

YEAR	TEAM	LVL	AGE	WHIP	ERA	DRA-	WARP	MPH	FB%	WHF	CSP
2018	ELP	AAA	24	1.20	3.45	75	0.8				
2018	SD	MLB	24	1.26	3.79	63	0.5	99.1	68.5%	36.6%	
2019	AMA	AA	25	4.50	54.00	159	0.0				
2019	ELP	AAA	25	0.30	0.00	24	0.2				
2019	SD	MLB	25	1.22	5.65	72	1.0	97.8	55.1%	36.4%	
2021 FS	*SD*	*MLB*	*27*	*1.40*	*4.27*	*96*	*0.3*	*98.0*	*57.2%*	*36.4%*	*46.0%*
2021 DC	*SD*	*MLB*	*27*	*1.40*	*4.27*	*96*	*0.1*	*98.0*	*57.2%*	*36.4%*	*46.0%*

Padres Prospects

The State of the System:

A strong farm system can help your big club in two ways. One, your prospects can turn into good major leaguers. Two, you can trade your prospects for good major leaguers. The Padres seem to have turned toward the second path.

The Top Ten:

─────── ★ ★ ★ *2021 Top 101 Prospect* **#10** ★ ★ ★ ───────

1

CJ Abrams SS OFP: 70 ETA: Late 2022/Early 2023
Born: 10/03/00 Age: 20 Bats: L Throws: R Height: 6'2" Weight: 185
Origin: Round 1, 2019 Draft (#6 overall)

The Report: Adley Rutschman was always going first overall in the 2019 draft, but Abrams was one of a handful of bats who were in the mix for the second pick. He "slid" to the Padres at six, and if you wanted to quibble with him last June, the bat perhaps didn't have the same upside as Bobby Witt Jr. or Riley Greene, and certainly lacked the safety of JJ Bleday or Andrew Vaughn. Abrams did offer plus-plus speed and the range and actions for shortstop, along with projectable hit and power combination. As soon as he landed in the complex though—and even accounting for the launching pads in Arizona—the bat looked much less like a laggard in the profile. While Abrams might never smash 20 home runs, fringe game power with plenty of doubles and triples looked more likely. The arm strength might be a bit light for shortstop—although his actions and quick release help it play up—but he'd be plus at second and has seen some time in center field as well, where his speed would be a significant asset.

Development Track: Abrams spent time at both the alternate site and instructs, where he looked about as much of a steal as a sixth overall pick can be. He's continued stinging the ball, driving plus major league velocity to the gaps consistently. It's still not entirely clear what his defensive landing home will be, but he could theoretically be average-or-better at all three up-the-middle spots. I'd expect him to start at Advanced-A next year and reach Double-A—and near the top of our 2022 prospect list—by the end of the year.

Variance: High. So it isn't a huge surprise that a top prep draft pick took a step forward in his first full pro season—or whatever this was—and moved from good prospect with some questions about the bat to top-ten-in-baseball type. However when your "first full pro season" was 2020, we are gonna keep the risk/variance factor on the high side.

Mark Barry's Fantasy Take: I'm not saying Abrams should be the No. 1 dynasty prospect, but I am saying that if he can keep doing what he's doing against more advanced pitching—that's the stuff No. 1 dynasty prospects are made of.

─────── ★ ★ ★ *2021 Top 101 Prospect* **#11** ★ ★ ★ ───────

2

MacKenzie Gore   LHP   OFP: 70   ETA: 2021
Born: 02/24/99   Age: 22   Bats: L   Throws: L   Height: 6'2"   Weight: 197
Origin: Round 1, 2017 Draft (#3 overall)

The Report: Gore entered the season as the best pitching prospect in baseball, and in our estimation he's still the best pitching prospect who hasn't made the majors yet. He has ace potential if he throws strikes and keeps developing. His fastball gets up into the mid-90s with late life. His curveball rates as plus-to-plus-plus, a majestic two-plane bender that he commands and tunnels extremely well. His slider is advanced, a tight above-average offering, and his changeup consistently also shows above-average. That's four above-average pitches or better. Except for blister issues and occasional wandering command, he's been the absolute total package in our live looks.

Development Track: Gore clearly should've made the majors this year given San Diego's pitching needs and his developmental timetable. He was repeatedly passed up for call-ups, although that could be the club being more comfortable using Luis Patiño and Ryan Weathers in relief. Because San Diego wasn't in the alternate site share and Gore didn't throw at instructs, there's basically no third-party scouting information available on him from the summer or fall. Dennis Lin of The Athletic talked to Gore in December and reported that he struggled during summer camp and fought his mechanics at the alternate site, which is broadly in line with industry scuttlebutt.

Variance: High. There's a lot of unanswered questions here. Gore could come firing bullets and make us look foolish for doubting him. Or he could not.

Mark Barry's Fantasy Take: Two things can be true: 1) Gore still has no-doubt, ace upside and 2) There are more questions about Gore today than there were last year at this time. It's a little concerning that he kept getting passed over for opportunities, but like Jarrett mentioned, that could just be the team not wanting to use him out of the 'pen. I might float some offers for Gore heading into 2021, to take the temperature of any managers skittish from his 2020 struggles. Even if he's not the best pitching prospect in baseball right now, he still could be a rotational anchor, and should be treated as such.

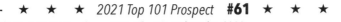

★ ★ ★ *2021 Top 101 Prospect* **#61** ★ ★ ★

3

Luis Campusano C   OFP: 60   ETA: Debuted in 2020
Born: 09/29/98   Age: 22   Bats: R   Throws: R   Height: 5'11"   Weight: 232
Origin: Round 2, 2017 Draft (#39 overall)

The Report: Campusano's offensive game is loud. The 2019 California League batting champion and co-MVP has the potential to hit for a significant average like you'd expect, and he has a very refined eye and plate approach. He barrels up and drives pitches, and while his power has been more gap-oriented so far, we think he's got the chance to get to above-average-to-plus game power as he further develops. Defensively, he has a strong arm, but needs to refine his overall throwing and receiving. He's a decent bet to stay at catcher, but doesn't currently project for defensive stardom; if he did, he'd be one of the top small handful of catching prospects in the game. He's not far off as-is.

Development Track: Campusano was called up in September and promptly smacked a homer in his first major-league game. He was scratched from his first start at catcher the next day and missed the rest of the regular season with a wrist injury, although he did pop back up as the third catcher on the postseason roster. In October, he was charged with felony marijuana possession after a traffic stop in Georgia. It is patently absurd that possession of slightly less than three ounces of weed constitutes a felony, to say nothing of broader systemic racial bias in the criminal justice system.

Variance: Medium, on skill.

Mark Barry's Fantasy Take: Going along with my "There Can Only Be One Dynasty Catcher" theory, I'm not stoked to pay a premium to acquire Campusano, as he's not Adley Rutschman. Still, if dynasty catchers are your thing, Campusano is neck-and-neck with Joey Bart for me as the next guy in line for the throne. There's a good offensive skill set here.

★ ★ ★ *2021 Top 101 Prospect* **#64** ★ ★ ★

4

Robert Hassell III CF   OFP: 60   ETA: 2023
Born: 08/15/01   Age: 19   Bats: L   Throws: L   Height: 6'2"   Weight: 195
Origin: Round 1, 2020 Draft (#8 overall)

The Report: The first high school player off the board in last year's draft, the Padres had their target in the crosshairs regardless of the presumptive best prep—Zac Veen—still being available. Hassell was as steady as they come throughout the evaluation process thanks to a swing and projected hit tool well beyond any others in his class. The sweet lefty stroke is balanced throughout and contains both contact and power potential to all fields. While that is certainly what grabbed the most attention, he is a better defender than given credit for, and was even considered a two-way prospect at one point. The arm off the mound worked in the low-90s and easily translates to either center or right field.

Development Track: If there's one thing you could copy-and-paste into virtually any of the players spotlighted it's that, "boy it sucked having them lose 2020 developmentally." If there were two things you could copy-and-paste to specifically the high schoolers from this (and any) draft, it's that Hassell will need to get into the weight room and fill out the rest of his frame. He's lean and strong as-is, but could stand to put on 10-15 pounds without losing a step.

Variance: Medium. The hitting ability and approach seems so good so early you just hope it's not messed with too much. It's fine to take some knocks, learn what works and what doesn't before making any big changes.

Mark Barry's Fantasy Take: It's always nice to be referred to as a pure hitter or having an advanced hit tool. It's better than the alternative at least. How that translates to fantasy typically depends on the other stuff in the profile. Can Hassell be discount Michael Brantley? Maybe. Is discount Michael Brantley just Melky Cabrera? Also maybe. I like Hassell as a top-75 name, but will need to see more (read: something) before going all in.

5 **Ryan Weathers LHP** OFP: 55 ETA: Debuted in 2020, sort of
Born: 12/17/99 Age: 21 Bats: R Throws: L Height: 6'1" Weight: 230
Origin: Round 1, 2018 Draft (#7 overall)

The Report: The son of righty bullpen stalwart David, Ryan Weathers is a lefty with a better chance to start than pops. The frame is a bit shorter and stouter, but Weathers repeats his slingy, uptempo, compact delivery well and can run his fastball up into the mid-90s. He also offers a potentially above-average curve and an average change. He mixes his stuff well and stays off barrels, so while he may lack a true bonafide out pitch, he does get a lot out of the current arsenal. Which is good, because given that stout frame, there isn't a ton of projection left.

Development Track: Like Alex Kirilloff and Shane McLanahan, Weathers found himself in the unusual circumstance of making his major-league debut in the playoffs. He was a bit of a surprise addition to the Padres' NLDS roster and immediately got some middle innings work in Game 1, showing a tick more on his fastball in the short burst outing. Granted, that's more info than we have on any Padres prospect who didn't show up in the majors or instructs. Weathers hasn't pitched above A-ball otherwise, and while he's not all that far off from the majors—he was an advanced arm for a prep pick—he'll likely start 2021 in Double-A, and the Friars' rotation is a bit more crowded now than it was last October.

Variance: High. Weathers is a 20-year-old pitching prospect with more present than projection, so we will have to see how that present plays in the near future in Double-A and higher.

Mark Barry's Fantasy Take: Oh hey, another Padres pitching prospect who got called up instead of Gore. I don't think Weathers has the stuff to be an impact starter in fantasy. If Weathers is going to have impact, it's going to be in the bullpen, and if Weathers pitches out of the bullpen, he's not really going to impact your fantasy lineup. Clear as mud? Good.

6 **Hudson Head** **CF** OFP: 55 ETA: 2023
Born: 04/08/01 Age: 20 Bats: L Throws: L Height: 6'1" Weight: 180
Origin: Round 3, 2019 Draft (#84 overall)

The Report: Head was a 2019 pop-up draft prospect who got overslot, late-first-round money from the Padres. He's a potential five-tool center fielder, but a lot of that is physical projection that might also move him to a corner. He has good bat speed and extension, and should be able to launch some baseballs as he fills out more. He's an above-average runner and an advanced defensive outfielder for his age. There's some tweenerish potential in the profile, but he's also a little bit safer than your median prep outfielder due to the present broad base of skills.

Development Track: Last year when we pegged Head as a potential big riser in the Padres' system for 2020, we expected it would be more due to further skill development then, uh, 10 or so guys ahead of him on the list being traded. His time at instructs was limited due to injury, but there were some positive reports on his bat.

Variance: High. Complex-league resume combined with some tweenerish signs and some stiffness in his load make for profile risk, but there's also the potential for five above-average tools in center field. That kind of profile plays up.

Mark Barry's Fantasy Take: This guy is pretty far away, but he has that nice blend of skills that could easily translate to a well-rounded fantasy profile. None of them really stand out as category carriers, however, so he's a watch list guy for me right now while we see how he fairs in full-season ball.

7 **Justin Lange** **RHP** OFP: 55 ETA: 2024 as a reliever, 2025 as a starter
Born: 09/11/01 Age: 19 Bats: R Throws: R Height: 6'4" Weight: 220
Origin: Round 1, 2020 Draft (#34 overall)

The Report: Lange is basically the inverse of fellow Texan Jared Kelley, who was long thought to be at-worst the second-best high school pitcher in the 2020 draft, but ended up falling to the 47th pick. Blessed with an ideal pitcher's frame, Lange shot up draft boards after adding close to 20 pounds of muscle during a six-month offseason period. What once was velocity in the low 90s was now up several ticks and hitting 100 on occasion during the spring. There is also some feel for a changeup that has a mimicking run similar to his fastball. In the inverse of the traditional prep arm, it's the breaking ball that is inconsistent. Like any rapidly maturing teenager, there isn't a ton of body control just yet and it shows in his command.

Development Track: Lange is a project pitcher. There's never-ending promise, but a lot of work to be done. The delivery in particular is worrisome, with a low slot that creates a lot of side spin to his pitches, it also puts a ton of stress on his elbow at the bottom of the arm swing and again with a recoiling follow-through at deceleration. He'll need to clean that up for his own long-term benefit while also finding something that he can comfortably repeat.

Variance: Extreme. There doesn't seem to be a ton of middle-ground/gray area in the profile. It will either all fall into place, or it won't. ---Keenan Lamb

Mark Barry's Fantasy Take: Lange has a bunch of stuff you look for in pitching prospects, but he's still a prep righty that hasn't thrown a professional pitch. That's not his fault, mind you, but I don't think you need to rush in for another couple years, at least.

8 **Jorge Oña   OF**   OFP: 50   ETA: Debuted in 2020
Born: 12/31/96   Age: 24   Bats: R   Throws: R   Height: 6'0"   Weight: 235
Origin: International Free Agent, 2016

The Report: Oña is a big man who wants to hit big bombs. Every time he is up at the plate the plan is swing hard, hit it 450. He gets to his power with a fairly short swing, but it's max effort and leveraged at the expense of barrel control or the ability to adjust to offspeed. That said, even his mishits can go for extra bases given how strong he is, and he has enough of an eye that he could get enough of all three outcomes to carry a corner outfield profile. Oña has the arm strength for right field, but his range and footspeed will be below-average in any outfield spot. He might be better suited for DH, assuming Rob Manfred works out whether or not there will be one in the National League in 2021 at some point.

Development Track: Oña got called up as an extra bat for a couple weeks in September. He struck out in almost half his plate appearances, but also hit one laser beam into the second deck at PetCo. He will need to balance the bombs and Ks a bit better going forward to be more than some fun pop off the bench, but given that he only has a month's worth of at-bats in Double-A—he missed most of 2019 after shoulder surgery—there's still time to work that out.

Variance: Medium. The K-rate may eat into enough of the hit tool—and with it some of the game power—that Oña is limited to pinch hitter with pop. But even marginal improvements on the swing-and-miss can lead to an exponential production boost based on how hard he can hit the ball when he does make contact.

Mark Barry's Fantasy Take: Oña back? An abbreviated 2019 Double-A breakout put Oña back onto the dynasty radar, culminating in a 2020 debut with the big club. There is a lot to like with this profile, but there are probably going to be too many strikeouts to feel comfortable rolling him out everyday.

9 **Reiss Knehr** **RHP** OFP: 50 ETA: Late 2021/Early 2022
Born: 11/03/96 Age: 24 Bats: L Throws: R Height: 6'2" Weight: 205
Origin: Round 20, 2018 Draft (#591 overall)

The Report: A Day 3 small college arm who didn't even get full pool, Knehr has had an uneven pro career despite pretty good stuff. He's a stocky righty with a delivery that starts a little drop and drive, but ends pretty upright, and there's effort throughout. So the command and control have been an issue even going back to college. He can run his fastball up in the mid-90s though, and has a pretty good cutter and changeup backing it up. Ultimately between the mechanics and shaky production as a pro starter, Knehr probably ends up in the 'pen, where the fastball/cutter combo might play up.

Development Track: Knehr pitched at instructs, where reports were better on the fastball velocity and secondaries, but until we see that translate into better outputs on his player page, the major league OFP here is going to be a little muted.

Variance: Medium. There's pretty significant reliever markers here, and it's not necessarily going to be late inning stuff in the pen unless it pops in short bursts. Yes, that usually happens, but it's not a guarantee.

Mark Barry's Fantasy Take: Knehr has the mix of a starter, but is probably destined for relief. Pass.

10 **Tucupita Marcano** **2B** OFP: 50 ETA: 2023
Born: 09/16/99 Age: 21 Bats: L Throws: R Height: 6'0" Weight: 170
Origin: International Free Agent, 2016

The Report: Marcano is a smooth infielder with an advanced approach and good feel for contact. The hit too projection is plus, contingent on him adding some more physical strength, but the game power will likely stall out at well-below-average. Marcano is a plus runner with the range for either middle infield spot—and he's played some third as a pro as well, but his arm strength would really only play at the keystone in an every day role.

Development Track: The Padres were reasonably aggressive with their prospects in 2020 and Marcano saw time at the alternate site and instructs. It's a slow burn profile given the slighter frame, and he will have to show harder contact against minor league pitching to project as more than a utility infielder.

Variance: High. Marcano has some skills that should give him some sort of major league career. He can hit, run, and play multiple infield spots. But he lacks physicality and we haven't really seen the bat tested by better arms yet.

Mark Barry's Fantasy Take: Normally, guys like Marcano are my jam. I love the heavy-contact, low-strikeout dudes that can run a little. Unfortunately, Marcano isn't all that efficient on the bases, snagging 15 bases in 31 tries in High-A. Love the bat--need to see more success in the base thievery.

The Prospects You Meet Outside The Top Ten

Prospects to dream on a little

Joshua Mears   **RF**   Born: 02/21/01   Age: 20   Bats: R   Throws: R   Height: 6'3"   Weight: 230   Origin: Round 2, 2019 Draft (#48 overall)

You would think a second-round prep outfielder in this subhead would be somewhat of a projection bet, and Mears will have to improve some things for sure. That said, he's already built like a major league right fielder in the midst of his physical prime. He has that kind of power too, although the swing is going to need a fair bit of fine tuning to get to it. He should be fine in right field and is a good runner for his size. It's going to need to click, and I don't know how likely that is, but you can dream on it.

Tirso Ornelas   **OF**   Born: 03/11/00   Age: 21   Bats: L   Throws: R   Height: 6'3"   Weight: 200   Origin: International Free Agent, 2017

Ornelas slides out of the Top Ten because he badly needed a consolidation year in the minors in 2020. The physical tools are among the best for position players in the system, but he's struggled with his swing and approach the last time we saw him in game action.

MLB bats, but less upside than you'd like

Eguy Rosario   **2B**   Born: 08/25/99   Age: 21   Bats: R   Throws: R   Height: 5'9"   Weight: 150   Origin: International Free Agent, 2015

Rosario is a future utility infielder that can handle all three spots and shows some feel for contact. The game power is limited, he probably won't get on base a ton, and he's swung and missed a little too much in two shots at the Cal League. He had a nice little instructs campaign, but the upside remains limited.

MLB arms, but probably relievers

Reggie Lawson   **RHP**   Born: 08/02/97   Age: 23   Bats: R   Throws: R   Height: 6'4"   Weight: 205   Origin: Round 2, 2016 Draft (#71 overall)

Lawson offers mid-90s heat and a potential plus hook, but our missing 2020 means that he hasn't been able to follow up on his rather electric 2019 AFL performance that itself followed an injury-marred regular season. We noted in last year's blurb that he was just 22, but next year he will be 24, so it might be time to move him to the pen and let him move quickly. He could be a boon to the Padres' 2021 relief corps.

You always need catching

Jonny Homza   **C**   Born: 06/13/99   Age: 22   Bats: R   Throws: R   Height: 6'0"   Weight: 185   Origin: Round 5, 2017 Draft (#138 overall)

Prep catchers are a risky proposition. Cold weather prep catchers? Even riskier. Well, it doesn't get much colder than Anchorage, Alaska. Homza, the first player ever drafted out of South Anchorage High School has taken a very conservative path through the minors and still hasn't seen full-season ball yet. He's a good defender though, and there's some projection in the bat that might be starting to bubble up after a good instructs.

Top Talents 25 and Under (as of 4/1/2021):

1. Fernando Tatis Jr., SS
2. C.J. Abrams, SS
3. MacKenzie Gore, LHP
4. Chris Paddack, RHP
5. Luis Campusano, C
6. Robert Hassell III, OF
7. Trent Grisham, OF
8. Adrian Morejon, LHP
9. Ryan Weathers, LHP
10. Hudson Head, OF

Fernando Tatis Jr. is one of the best young players in baseball. He's an emerging two-way superstar who hits for average, hits for power, and makes some fantastic plays at shortstop. There isn't even much more to say.

Chris Paddack could really, really use a workable third pitch. As a fastball/changeup starter, the league has seemed to catch up to him multiple times through, and he's had a harder time inducing whiffs and weak contacts. His curveball isn't getting there, and he introduced a cutter late in 2020. If he can figure out something that breaks gloveside, he still could be a top-of-the-rotation starter.

Trent Grisham's DRC+ numbers (90 in Milwaukee in 2019, 95 in San Diego in 2020) have not lived up to his slash line (.243/.342/.437 career) so far, but they're still usable. The speedster has settled in in center field and looked great out there in 2020, and even at a slightly below-average DRC+ he's a nifty regular as long as that's true.

Adrian Morejon graduated on service time in 2020 after spending the second half of August and all of September bouncing between being an opener and a long reliever. He gave up an absolute boat load of homers (7 in 19 1/3 innings), though the stuff was still pretty good and his DRA was slightly above-average. Our concerns about whether he has enough command and durability to start remain, but even in a shorter role he's on the way to being a nifty weapon.

Part 3: Featured Articles

Padres All-Time Top 10 Players

by Steven Goldman

POSITION PLAYERS

GENE TENACE, C/1B (1977-1980)

A three-true outcomes demigod whose statistics were diminished by the era and the parks in which he played. Tenace played in five postseasons with the A's, winning the World Series MVP with four home runs in 1972. Joining the Padres as a free agent in 1977, he was almost the exact same hitter he had been in Oakland. He still was excellent at reaching base at Jack Murphy Stadium (.233/.401/.382) but the power was only seen by fans on the road (.242/.404/.461). He was considered a disappointment, but only Winfield outhit him during his four years with the team. Actual first name was "Fury."

NATE COLBERT, 1B (1969-1974)

Colbert was doubly damaged by the Astros organization before being chosen by the Padres in the 1968 expansion draft. First they tore him away from his hometown Cardinals during the Rule 5 draft and sat him on the bench for a full year despite his lack of experience above the lower minors. Subsequently he became of many players of color given short shrift by that organization during the Harry Walker era. Over his first five years in San Diego, Colbert hit .260/.333/.483 with 149 home runs, twice totaling 38. As with almost every player on this list, his power was curtailed by the Padres' ballpark and given a different environment he would have surpassed 40 home runs on more than one occasion despite playing in what was generally a low-offense era. Back problems rapidly curtailed his career thereafter and he was out of the majors at 31.

ADRIAN GONZALEZ, 1B (2006-2010)

Acquired by the Padres after two organizations had given up on him, Gonzalez quickly shed the bust label as well as questions about his power production, hitting .304/.362/.500. He continued to improve throughout his San Diego stay, becoming one of the few Padres to hit 40 home runs in 2009. Traded to the Red Sox on the verge of free agency, he remains a testament to the tough hitting environment of his old team: His .288/.374/.514 rates with the Padres breaks down to .307/.381/.579 while eating room service, .267/.367/.442 when cooking in his own kitchen.

KEN CAMINITI, 3B (1997-1998)

One of the game's most tragic stories. Caminiti came up with the Astros in 1987 and proved to be an indifferent offensive player, hitting only .247/.304/.348 through his age-28 season. After that he got much better, hitting .289/.370/.500 over the next nine years and approximately 1,100 games. That included, in 1996 with the Padres, one of the best seasons ever recorded by a major league third baseman. He hit .326/.408/.521 with 40 home runs. He won the NL MVP award. The performance was not entirely the result of hard work, but of performance-enhancing drugs. It turned out that wasn't the extent of his pharmaceutical experiments—he was also using cocaine and heroin. The latter substances killed him at the age of 41, six years after he'd departed the Padres as a free agent to re-sign with the Astros.

PHIL NEVIN, 3B/OF (1999-2005)

The Astros made Nevin the first-overall pick of the 1992 draft, watched him struggle through a couple of mediocre seasons as Triple-A, then dealt him to the Tigers in return for six weeks of an aging Mike Henneman. It took another couple of trades and even a desperation move to catcher before Nevin finally broke through with the Padres in 1999. From 2000-2001 he hit .304/.381/.565. In the latter season he hit 41 home runs and drove in 126 runs. Within a few years age began to catch up to him, but he remains one of four Padres with a .500 career slugging percentage during his stay with the team.

CHASE HEADLEY, 3B (2007-2013, 2018)

Initially stuck in left field because he was blocked at third by Kevin Kouzmanoff, Headley finally got his chance to play third in his third major-league season. He proved to be a good glove but an odd offensive player, one who hit 12, 4, 31, and 13 home runs in consecutive seasons. He never did re-scale the heights of 2012, in which he hit .286/.376/.498 with the aforementioned 31 homers, drew 86 walks, led the NL in RBI, and won the Gold Glove. Traded to the Yankees and signed to a contract extension Brian Cashman had immediate cause to regret, he failed to hit at even a league-average level and his career ended almost as soon as the contract did.

DAVE WINFIELD, OF (1973-1980)

A fantastic all-around athlete coveted by the major leagues in three different sports, Winfield claimed not to have heard of the Padres when they made him the fourth-overall pick of the 1973 draft (the Rangers, Phillies, and Brewers past, though it's hard to fault the latter for going after Robin Yount). The 6-foot-6 outfielder jumped right to the majors and basically never struggled, although it took a few years for him to round into peak form. He hit "only" 465 home runs in his career because he never played in a park conducive to his skills. That included Jack Murphy Stadium, where he hit .271/.346/.445 versus .296/.368/.481 on the road.

GENE RICHARDS, OF (1977-1983)

Because the Padres have often had trouble acquiring and/or retaining great players until recently, it takes just a few great seasons to get on the list. The first-overall pick in the now-defunct January phase of the draft in 1975 (his college teammate Willie Mays Aikens was second), Richards was a speed and patience player who arguably should have made an All-Star team or two. He hit .294/.365/.392 over his first five seasons while stealing up to 61 bases a season. A serious knee injury in 1982 diminished his chief skill and his career ended quickly.

TONY GWYNN, OF (1982-2001)

Gwynn, Boggs, Ichiro, Carew. These were great precisions players of a style whose presence in the game is greatly missed. Gwynn amassed seven batting tiles and made a serious run at .400 in 1994 before labor shenanigans ended the season. A pioneer in the use of video to refine his swing, Gwynn struck out just 434 times in his career or 29 times per 162 games played, a standard that seems impossible now. Born in Los Angeles, a product of San Diego State University, that Gwynn was still available to be selected by the Padres in the third round of the 1981 draft (after they had taken Kevin McReynolds, Frank Castro, and Bill Long) seems like fate. He had some of the fastest hands seen in the modern major leagues, giving him the ability to adjust to pitches on any part of the plate and drive them. Fast enough to reach double-figures in triples our times and steal up to 56 bases, the only knock on him was that he struggled to keep his weight down. As the years and pounds increased, his speed decreased and a player who had been a four-time Gold Glover became a defensive liability. In fighting his waistline, Gwynn was like many of us. In all other regards he was unique.

BRIAN GILES, OF (2003-2009)

Timing is everything and if Giles had been drafted by any team other than Cleveland at a moment when their outfield was jammed with talent (Albert Belle, Kenny Lofton, Manny Ramirez) he might well have amassed Hall of Fame-level career statistics. As it was, he was an unusual hitter, capable of high contact relative to his era but also selective, drawing 90 or more walks seven times in his career. He had power too, poking up to 39 home runs in a season. The result was both a career .400 on-base percentage and career .500 slugging percentage. Only 27 players have done that since 1900 (1000 or more games). Aside from two who are active (Mike Trout and Joey Votto) and one who is ineligible (Shoeless Joe Jackson) 17 of the remaining 25 have plaques. That's not an argument for Giles' enshrinement given some of his off-the-field issues, but only goes to show that the Padres got the tail end of a special career.

PITCHERS

RANDY JONES, LHP (1973-1980)

A workhorse sinker-slider pitcher, Jones rarely struck batters out with his slow-moving stuff (his career rate was 3.4 whiffs per nine) but was effective nevertheless because he induced weak contact. After going 8-22 with a 4.45 ERA that was more reflective of his reliance on a weak defense than the effectiveness of his approach in 1974, he changed his mechanics, cut his walk rate nearly in half, and went 20-12 with a league-leading 2.24 ERA. He finished second to Tom Seaver in the Cy Young Award balloting but claimed the trophy for himself in 1976 with a league-leading 22 wins and a 2.74 ERA in 315.1 innings, 40 starts, and 25 complete games. (The 1986 World Series wasn't the first time manager John McNamara showed a reluctance to make an in-game change.) His arm never quite recovered, although he was a reasonably effective pitcher in 1978 and 1979.

ERIC SHOW, RHP (1981-1990)

A troubled, tragic man whose life ended before his 38th birthday, Show was a good pitcher who deserves to be remembered for more than giving up Pete Rose's record-breaking hit in 1985 or the way his life unraveled thereafter. A hard thrower by the standards of the early 1980s with good command, he wasn't, pardon the expression, showy. There's no black ink on his baseball card, nothing that stands out except stolid effectiveness. "Show has intelligence going for him," the Scouting Report: 1985 opined. "He is a student of philosophy, religion and physics, and some people try to explain his bad outings by saying he 'thinks too much on the mound.' That, of course is a shallow argument." It was shallow because he wasn't thinking too much on the mound but thinking everywhere in patterns that led to addiction and self-destructive behavior. Baseball is a microcosm not just of our society, but sometimes of our very lives. Show revealed himself before the world, but you had to get past the on-field results to see it.

ED WHITSON, RHP (1983-1984, 1986-1991)

Whitson wasn't overpowering, throwing a 90-mph fastball and a 55-mph palmball. He had good control, walking few batters, and he was stingy with the home runs. He'd passed through Pittsburgh, San Francisco, and Cleveland, mostly unhappily—he thought he should be a rotation fixture, but he tended to get pushed into a swingman role. The Padres let him pitch in the way he wanted to and they were rewarded as he helped pitch them to the 1984 World Series with a 14-8, 3.24-ERA season in 1984. That winter he took George Steinbrenner's money, a colossal mistake for all involved that led to a year and a half of all-around misery—Whitson was a quiet man from Tennessee and he was ill-suited to pitching in New York, but in fairness he was also treated poorly by both Yankees fans, who harassed him and his family, and the organization itself. Traded back to San Diego in July, 1986, he was slow to regain his form, but was terrific in 1989 and 1990, going 30-20 with a 2.63 ERA in 65 starts.

GREG W. HARRIS, RHP (1988-1993)

The quickest way to destroy a pitcher c. 1993 was to trade him to the expansion Colorado Rockies. Prior to that July 1993 transaction, Harris had been a very effective pitcher for the Padres in a limited role, pitching out of the bullpen or as a swingman. Though he was basically a two-pitch pitcher, general manager Joe McIlvaine was inspired to move him to the starting rotation in 1991. After a half-season pause for elbow problems, the plan proceeded. Harris made 20 starts and turned in a 2.23 ERA. Overall, he had a 2.34 ERA in 403.1 innings. That was the last good year of his career. He made another 20 starts in 1992, another season disrupted by injury, and this time the results were poor. The trade to the Rockies followed and decency prevents us from saying more.

BRUCE HURST, LHP (1989-1993)

Take a veteran left-handed pitcher out of Fenway Park, put him in a league without the designated hitter, and don't be surprised if you get good results, but not this good. After nine seasons with the Red Sox, Hurst joined the Padres as a free agent. He was in his 30s and had already pitched nearly 1500 major league innings. In short, youth had flown. Yet, in the four healthy seasons Hurst had with the Padres, he turned in a 3.22 ERA, more than a full run below his career mark with the Red Sox. He'd always been an intelligent pitcher, changing his speeds and spotting his fastball well, but now he was in an environment that worked with him instead of against him. The inevitable arm problems began to creep in towards the end of the run and the Padres packed him off to the Rockies (with Greg Harris) as he was coming off rotator cuff surgery, which was just cruel.

ANDY BENES, RHP (1989-1995)

The Padres made college hurler Benes the first-overall pick of the 1988 draft and he rewarded them by pitching his way to the big leagues by the following August. He never became an ace but he had many solid years at the journeyman-plus/occasional All-Star level (he made the team in 1993), striking out batters with his low-90s fastball (a more impressive velocity then than now). He led the NL in strikeouts and strikeout rate in 1994, but, as was par for the course with the Padres in those days, he also led the league in losses due to weak run support. Reached the 230-inning mark three times around the shortened 1994-1995 seasons and got there a fourth time in 1998; by today's standards that makes him practically Iron Man McGinnity.

ANDY ASHBY, RHP (1993-1999)

Ashby had an unlikely journey to becoming a Padres All-Star in 1998 and 1999. Signed by the Phillies as a non-drafted free agent, he pitched his way to the majors by 1991, fighting his control the entire time. Despite miserable results, he was selected by the Rockies in the 1992 expansion draft. He then spent most of three months being ruthlessly thrashed as part of Colorado's inaugural season. Padres scouts must have seen something they liked, though, because they traded for him in July. And yet, the thrashing continued; at season's end, Ashby's career record was 5-18 with a 6.77 ERA in 202 innings. From that moment until the end of his Padres phase he went 67-56 with a 3.49 ERA. He became more aggressive, cutting his walk rate and challenging hitters with his sinking fastball. He wasn't exactly dominating; he just became the maximum version of himself his skills would allow. The intersection of scouting, coaching, environment, and a player's own level of maturity is complex, but Ashby was one of the rare players who through some combination of luck and perseverance landed squarely where those four corners meet.

TREVOR HOFFMAN, RHP (1993-2008)

The one-time career saves leader was drafted by the Reds as a shortstop. He had the arm for the position but not the bat, and after two years the organization moved him to the mound. He had almost instant success, whiffing 14 batters per nine in his first season as a pitcher. Before the Reds could call him up he was drafted by the Marlins in the 1993 expansion draft. He made his major league debut that April and two months later was traded to the Padres when they deaccessioned Gary Sheffield. He took over the closer's role the next season and didn't relinquish it for roughly 15 years, the sole exception coming in 2003 when he missed all but nine games due to shoulder surgery. The secret to his longevity was one of the great changeups; a pitcher can survive declining velocity as long as there's some spread between his fastball and his change. Hoffman managed that transition as well as anyone, remaining effective into his early 40s.

JOEY HAMILTON, RHP (1994-1998)

The Padres don't have a great history picking pitchers in draft's first round. Hamilton, who they tabbed with the eighth-overall pick in 1991, is an example of a selection who wasn't a bust but also was far from an ace. Hamilton utilized a sinking fastball to induce grounders. His first two seasons (1994 and 1995) teased greater success to come with a 3.05 ERA in 313 innings, but a pitcher whose strikeout rate is generally below average can't afford to right his command. Hamilton increasingly did, walking more batters in his fifth major league season (4.4 per nine, a league-leading 106 overall) than he did when he reached the majors.

JAKE PEAVY, RHP (2002-2009)

The 2007 NL Cy Young Award winner was thought to be committed to Auburn when the Padres called his name in the 15th round of the 1999 draft. It turned out Peavy had an open mind about being a college man and signed. He overmatched the low minors as a teenager and reached the majors at 21. By 23 he had found his command and had won the first of his two ERA titles, and the year after that he led the NL in strikeouts, also for the first of two times. He never had a true off year for the rest of his Padres stay, though he did pitch in very poor luck in 2006, putting up a 4.09 ERA that in no way matched his peripherals. On the verge of his contract ending in 2009 and showing the first signs of what would be frequent injury problems, the Padres dealt him to the White Sox.

A Taxonomy of 2020 Abnormalities

by Rob Mains

I'm going to start this with a trivia question. Trust me, it's relevant. Don't bother skipping to the end of the article to find the answer, it's not there.

Only five players have appeared in 140 or more games for 16 straight seasons. Who are they?

It's a trivia question starting off an essay, so you know how this works: Whatever you guessed, you're wrong. It's okay. As someone who purchased this book, chances are good that you're an educated baseball fan. But the circumstances behind 2020 force us to abandon, or at least seriously question, some of our favorite patterns and crutches for evaluating the game we love.

We just completed what was undoubtedly the strangest season in MLB history. No fans, geographically limited schedule, universal DH, seven-inning twin bills, runners on second in extra innings, a 16-team postseason, a club playing at a Triple-A stadium. Some of these changes will likely persist (sorry), but we've never had so many tweaks dumped on us all at once, at least not since they figured out how many balls were in a walk.

And the biggest, of course, was the 60-game season. The 19th century was dotted with teams that went bankrupt before the season ended, but the lone season with only 60 scheduled games was 1877. That year there were only six teams, the league rostered a total of 77 players (just 16 more than the 2020 Marlins), and batters called for pitches to be thrown high or low by the pitcher, who was 50 feet away. We can say the 2020 season was easily the shortest ever for recognizable baseball.

As such, it'll stand out. Few abbreviated seasons do. Just about everybody reading this knows the 1994 season ended after Seattle's Randy Johnson struck out Oakland's Ernie Young for the last out of the Mariners-A's game on August 11. The ensuing player strike wiped out the rest of the season and the postseason. Teams played only 112-117 games that year.

And many of you know that a strike in the middle of the 1981 season split the season in two, resulting in the only Division Series until 1995. Teams played only 103-111 games that year, the shortest regular season since 1885.

Those two seasons are memorable. So when we see that nobody drove in 100 runs in 1981, or that Greg Maddux was the only pitcher with 180 or more innings pitched in 1994, we think, "Of course. Strike year."

But we don't remember other short years. You might not recall that the 1994 strike spilled into the next year, chopping 18 games off the 1995 schedule. You might've read that the 1918 season, played during the last pandemic, ended after Labor Day due to the government's World War I "work or fight" order. A strike erased the first week and a half of the 1972 season, but that year's best known as the last time pitchers batted in the American League.

The point is, while we don't remember small changes to the schedule, we remember the big ones. The 1981 mid-season strike. The 1994 season- and Series-ending strike. And, of course, the pandemic-shortened 2020 season. We won't need a reminder why Marcell Ozuna's 18 homers were the fewest to lead the National League in a century. (Literally; Cy Williams led with 15 in 1920.)

Now, about that trivia question. The five players are Hank Aaron, Brooks Robinson, Pete Rose, Ichiro Suzuki, and Johnny Damon. The one nobody gets, of course, is Damon, and a lot of people miss Ichiro, whose last season of 140-plus games came garbed in the red-orange and ocean blue of Miami when he was 42. That's half of what makes it a good question. The other half is the two guys whom many think made the list but didn't. Lou Gehrig? His streak started in the Yankees' 42nd game of the 1925 season and lasted only 13 seasons after that. And everybody assumes Cal Ripken Jr. did it, having played 2,632 straight games over 17 seasons. But one of those 17 seasons was 1994, when the Orioles played only 112 games.

My point? *I just told you* everybody remembers the 1994 strike year, but everybody forgets it fell in the middle of Ripken's streak, separating the first twelve years from the last four. Just because we recall something doesn't mean it's always at the front of our minds.

Nobody is going to forget 2020, and baseball is obviously not the main reason. But there will come a time in the future when you're looking at a player's or a team's record, and there will be baffling numbers there for 2020, and you'll think, "I wonder what happened." (Not to mention the missing line for minor league players.) Just like you forgot that the 1994 strike limited Ripken to 112 games.

Try not to forget it, though. The 2020 season resulted in weird statistical results for several reasons.

There were only 60 games.
I know, duh. But that had impacts beyond counting stats like Ozuna's home run total or Yu Darvish and Shane Bieber leading the majors with eight wins. (I know, pitcher wins, but still.)

The 162-game season is the longest among major North American sports, and that duration gives us a gift. Over the course of a long season, small variations tend to even out. A player who has a ten-game hot streak will probably have a ten-game cold streak. A team that starts the year losing a bunch of close games will probably win a bunch of them. We get regression to the mean. Statistics stabilize.

Consider flipping a coin. Over the long run, we expect it to come up heads about half the time. But the fewer flips, the more variation there'll be. If you flip a coin six times, probability theory tells us you'll get at least two-third heads about 34 percent of the time. Flip it 30 times, your chance of two-thirds heads drops to five percent.

Or, relevant to this case, if you flip a coin 60 times, your chance of getting at least 36 heads—that's 60 percent—is 7.75 percent. Expand the coin-flipping to 162 times, and the chance of getting 60 percent heads drops to 0.73 percent.

In other words, the odds of an outcome that's 20 percent better (or worse) than expected is *more than ten times higher* when you flip your coin 60 times than when you do it 162 times. Call it small sample size, call lack of mean reversion, or call it luck not evening out, 162 is a lot more predictive than 60. You get much more variation over 60 games than over 162. Bieber's 1.63 ERA and 0.87 FIP aren't something we'd see over a full season, and neither is Javier Baéz's .203/.238/.360.

Some players' lines in 2020 look normal. Brian Anderson had an .811 OPS in 2019 and an .810 OPS in 2020. (He probably would have gotten that last point if he'd been given enough time.) But there are many like Bieber and Baéz, some of them from young players still establishing their talent levels. The answer to the question, "What went right or wrong for that guy in 2020?" is most likely "Nothing, it was just a 2020 thing."

Preseason training was abbreviated for hitters.

Every year, spring training drags. Players get tired of it, fans get tired of it, and you sure can tell sportswriters get tired of it. Yes, something to get everyone into shape is necessary, but does it really have to drag on for over a month? Can't we shorten it?

The 2020 season answered in the negative, at least for hitters. Warren Spahn is credited with saying that hitting is timing and pitching is upsetting timing. It appears nobody had his timing down after the abbreviated July summer camp. Through August 9—18 games into the season—MLB batters were hitting .230/.311/.395 with a .275 BABIP. That BABIP, had it held, would have been the lowest since 1968, the Year of the Pitcher. In recent years it's hovered around .300.

It didn't hold. Play returned to more normal levels the rest of the year: .249/.325/.425 with a .297 BABIP starting August 10. But batters whose play concentrated in those first two weeks wound up with ugly lines. Andrew

Benintendi went on the injured list with a season-ending rib cage strain on August 11. His final line: .103/.314/.128 in 14 games. Franchy Cordero went on the IL with a hamate bone fracture on August 9 and a .154/.185/.231 line. Even though he came back strong in a late September return, it was too late to repair his full-season numbers.

Preseason training was abbreviated for pitchers.

Every year, spring training drags. Players get tired of it, fans get tired of it ... wait, I already said that. But the abbreviated preseason was tough on pitchers, too. As noted, they had the upper hand coming out of the gate. But then they lost that hand. And then their arms, too.

The 2020 season was spread over 67 days. During those 67 days, 237 pitchers hit the Injured List, compared to 135 in the first 67 days of 2019. A lot of those IL stints, though, were COVID-19-related. Still, over the first 67 days of the 2019 season, there were 72 pitchers on the IL with arm injuries. That figure jumped to 110 in 2020, a 53 percent increase.

There are a number of factors contributing to pitcher arm injuries, ranging from usage to velocity, but it appears that attenuated preseason training played a role. A lot of pitchers had super-short seasons due to arm woes. Corey Kluber, Roberto Osuna, and Shohei Ohtani combined for seven innings, none after August 8. All suffered arm injuries. We'll never know whether they'd have fared better with a longer preseason, but we can guess how they probably feel.

Everybody played.

Rosters were set to expand from 25 to 26 in 2020, so even if we'd had a normal season, we'd have likely seen 2019's record of 1,410 players on MLB rosters broken. But due to the pandemic, rosters started the year at 30 and were cut to only 28. Add multiple COVID-19 absences and the revolving door caused by poor starts by hitters and a rash of pitcher arm injuries, and 1,289 players appeared in MLB games in 2020. The comparable figure over the first 67 days of the 2019 season was 1,109. That 16 percent increase works out to an average of six more players per team in 2020 compared to a similar slice of 2019. A future look back at 2020 rosters will include a lot of unfamiliar names.

Plus became a minus.

In advanced metrics, we adjust batter and pitcher performance for park and league/era variations. A plus sign appended to the end of a measure means that it's adjusted for park and league. It's scaled to an average of 100, with higher figures above average and lower figures below average. (Similarly, a metric with a minus is also park- and league-adjusted and scaled to 100, with lower values better.) Here at BP, our advanced measure of offensive performance is DRC+. Baseball-Reference has OPS+ and FanGraphs has wRC+.

Using park and league adjustments, we can compare Dante Bichette's 1995 Steroid Era season at pre-humidor Coors Field (.340/.364/.620, 40 homers, 128 RBI, MVP runner-up) with Jim Wynn's 1968 Year of the Pitcher season at the cavernous Astrodome (.269/.376/.474, 26 homers, 67 RBI, no MVP votes). It's not close. DRC+, OPS+, and wRC+ all give the nod to Wynn, handily. This is a useful tool. As my Baseball Prospectus colleague Patrick Dubuque tweeted last fall, "Please note that when I ask how you are, I am already adjusting for era."

The 2020 season messes up plus (and minus) stats for two reasons. First, the park adjustment was based on only 30 home games instead of the usual 81. Everything noted above regarding the short season applies, literally doubly, to park effect calculations. DRC+ uses a single-season park factor. OPS+ uses a three-year average and wRC+ five years. The figure for 2020 is suspect.

Second, OPS+ and wRC+ adjust for league: American and National. (DRC+ adjusts for opponent, regardless of league.) While there were two leagues in 2020, they were an artificial construct. To reduce travel, teams played opponents geographically, not based on league. There weren't two leagues, American and National. There were three, Western, Central, and Eastern.

That makes a difference because teams in the same league played in different run-scoring environments. AL teams scored 4.58 runs per game, NL teams 4.71. That's a small difference. But teams in the East scored 0.21 more runs per game (4.95) than teams in the West (4.74), and they both scored a lot more than Central teams (4.25). Adjusting for league misses that difference, so this book will be safe in that regard, but other sources may be distorted somewhat.

Not every game was a "game."

In 2020, the rising tide of strikeouts was finally stemmed. Strikeouts per team per game fell from 8.8 in 2019 to 8.7 in 2020. That marked the first decline after 14 straight annual increases.

In 2020, the rising tide of strikeouts rose higher. Batters struck out in 23.4 percent of plate appearances compared to 23.0 percent in 2019. That marked the 15th straight annual increase.

Both are true statements.

Because of two rule changes—seven-inning doubleheaders and runners on second in extra innings—games in 2020 were unprecedented in their brevity. There were 37.0 plate appearances per game in 2020. The only years with fewer were 1904 and 1906-1909. The average game in 2020 entailed 8.61 innings pitched, the fewest since 1899.

So when you see any per-game stats for 2020, you need to increase them by 3 or 4 percent to get them on equal footing with recent years.

Or, better, just ignore them. Last year happened. There were major league games contested between major league teams. But when you're looking at those physical or electronic baseball cards, when you're weaving narratives over why this young player's inevitable rise to stardom fell apart or why that old veteran rekindled his magic, don't linger on the 2020 line. It was just too weird. ▪

Thanks to Lucas Apostoleris for research assistance.

—Rob Mains is an author of Baseball Prospectus.

Tranches of WAR

by Russell A. Carleton

We ask "replacement level" to be a lot of things. Sometimes contradictory things. Sometimes I wonder if we know what it even means anymore. The original idea was that it represented the level of production that a team could expect to get from "freely available talent", including bench players, minor leaguers, and waiver wire pickups. It created a common benchmark to compare everyone to, and for that reason, it represented an advancement well beyond what was available at the time. In fact, it created a language and a framework for evaluating players that was not just better but *entirely* different than what came before it.

But then we started mumbling in that language. The idea behind "wins above replacement" was one part sci-fi episode and one part mathematical exercise. Imagine that a player had disappeared before the season and suddenly, in an alternate timeline, his team would have had to replace him. The distance between him and that replacement line was his value. We need to talk about that alternate timeline.

Without getting too into 2:00 am "deep conversations" with extensive navel-gazing, it's worth thinking about why one player might not be playing, while another might.

- A player might not be playing because he has a short-term injury or his manager believes that he needs a day off.
- A player might not be playing because he has a longer-term injury that requires him to be on the injured list.

There's a difference here between these two situations. In particular, the first one generally *doesn't* involve a compensatory roster move, while the second one does. It's possible, though not guaranteed, that the person who will be replacing the injured/resting player would be the same in either case. That matters. Teams generally carry a spare part for all eight position players on the diamond, although in the era of a four-player bench, those spare parts usually are the backup plan for more than one spot.

111

A couple of years ago, I posed a hypothetical question. Suppose that a team had two players in its system fighting for a fourth outfielder spot. One of them was a league average hitter, but would be worth 20 runs below average if allowed to play center field for a full season. One of them was a perfectly average fielder, but would be 15 runs below average as a hitter, if allowed to play an entire season. Which of the two should the team roster? It's tempting to say the second one, as overall, he is the better player. That misses the point. A league average hitter on the bench isn't just a potential replacement for an injured outfielder. He might also pinch hit for the light-hitting shortstop in a key spot. You keep the average hitter on the roster, even though he isn't a hand-in-glove fit for one specific place on the field, because being a bench player is a different job description than being a long-term fill-in for someone. If you find yourself in need of a longer-term fill-in, you can bring the other guy up from AAA.

When we're determining the value of an everyday player though, if he had disappeared before the season and a team would have had to replace his production, they likely would have done it with a player who was a long-term fill-in type because they would have had to replace a guy who played everyday. Maybe that's the same guy that they would have rostered on their bench anyway, but we don't know. It gets to the query of what we hope to accomplish with WAR. Are we looking for an accurate modeling of reality or are we looking for a common baseline to compare everyone to? Both have their uses, but they are somewhat different questions.

Let's talk about another dichotomy.

- A player might not be playing because he isn't very good and is a bench-level player.
- A player might not be playing because there is another player on the team who has a situational advantage that makes him the better choice today. The classic case of this is a handedness platoon. On another day, he might be a better choice.

When we think about player usage, I think we're still stuck in the model that there are starters and there are scrubs. We have plenty of words for bench players or reserves or backups or utility guys. We do still have the word "platoon" in our collective vocabulary, but in the age of short benches, it's hard to construct one. It's always been hard to construct them. You have to find two players who hit with different hands, have skill sets that complement each other, and probably play the same position. In the era of the short bench, one of them had probably better double as a utility player in some way. Baseball has a two-tiered language geared toward the idea of regulars and reserves. The fact that it was so easy for me to find plenty of synonyms for "a player whose primary function is to come into a game to replace a regular player if he is injured or resting" should tell you something.

I'm always one to look for "unspoken words" in baseball. What is it called when someone is both half of a platoon and the utility infielder? That guy exists sometimes, but he reveals himself in that role—usually by accident. We don't have a word for that, and whenever I find myself saying "we don't have a word for that", I look for new opportunities. What do you call it, further, when the job of being the utility infielder is decentralized across the whole infield with occasional contributions from the left fielder? It's not even a "super-utility" player. What happens when you build your entire roster around the idea that everyone will be expected to be a triple major?

⚾   ⚾   ⚾

I think someone else beat me to this one, and on a grand scale. Platoons work because we know that hitters of the opposite hand to the pitcher get better results than hitters of the same hand, usually to the tune of about 20 points of OBP. If you want to express that in runs, it usually comes out to somewhere around 10 to 12 runs of linear weights value prorated across 650 PA. But hang on a second, now let's say that we have two players who might start today, both of roughly equal merit with the bat. One has a handedness advantage, but is the worse fielder of the two. In that case, as long as his "over the course of a season" projection as a fielder at whatever position you want to slot him into is less than a 10-run drop from the guy he might replace, then he's a better option today.

We're not used to thinking of utility players as bat-first options, who would play below-average defense at three different infield positions. That guy might hook on as a 2B/3B/LF type (Howie Kendrick, come on down!) but teams usually think to themselves that they need as their utility infielder someone who "can handle" shortstop, the toughest of the infield spots to play. If someone can do that *and* hit well, he's probably already starting somewhere, so he's not available as a utility infielder. It's easier for those glove guys to find a job. In a world where the replacement for a shortstop *has to be* the designated utility infielder, that makes sense.

But as we talked about last week, we're living in a different world. The rate at which a replacement for a regular starter turns out to be *another starter* shifting over to cover has gone way up over the last five years. There was always some of it in the game, but this has been a supernova of switcheroos. Now if your second baseman is capable of playing a decent shortstop, that 2B/3B/LF guy can swap in. He's not actually playing shortstop, and maybe the defense suffers from the switch, but if he's got enough of a bat, he might outhit those extra fielding miscues. And in doing so, he is effectively your backup shortstop.

Somewhere along the lines, teams got hip to the idea of multi-positional play from their regulars. I've written before about how you can't just put a player, however athletic, into a new position and expect much at first. The data tell us that. Eventually, players can learn to be multi-positionalists, but it takes time, roughly on the order of two months, before they're OK. But there's a hidden message in there. If you give a player some reps at a new spot, he's a reasonably gifted athlete and somewhat smart and willing to learn, he could probably pick it up enough to get to "good enough," and it doesn't take forever. You just have to be purposeful about it. Maybe you get to the point where you can start to say "he's still below average but we could move him there and get another bat into the lineup, and it's a net win."

Teams have started to build those extra lessons into their player development program. It used to be seen as a mark of weakness to be relegated to "utility player" because that meant that you were a bench player (all those synonyms above come with a side of stigma). Now, it's a way of building a team. If you get a few reps in the minors (where it doesn't count) at a spot, you'll have at least played the spot at game speed before. There are limits to how far you can push that. A slow-footed "he's out in left field because we don't have the DH" guy is never going to play short, but maybe your third baseman can try second base and not look like a total moose out there.

Ⓧ   Ⓧ   Ⓧ

Back to WAR. I'd argue that the world of starters and scrubs is slowly disintegrating, for good cause. In the event that a regular starter really does go down with an injury–ostensibly, the alternate universe scenario that WAR is attempting to model–it makes the team a little more resilient to replacing him. And the good news is that you're more likely to be able to replace him with the best of the bench bunch, rather than the third-best guy, because the best guy doesn't have to be an exact positional match for the guy who got hurt. And that's what the manager would want to do. He'd want to replace that long-term production, not with an amalgam of everyone else who played that position, but with the best guy available from his reserves.

Now this is still WAR. We still want to retain the principle that we should be measuring a player, and not his teammates. We need some sort of common baseline, and despite what I just said, we'll still need some sort of amalgam. To construct that, I give to you the idea of the tranche. The word, if you've not heard it before, refers to a piece of a whole that is somehow segmented off. It's often used in finance to talk about layers of a financial instrument.

Here, I want you to consider that there are 30 starters at each of the seven non-battery positions (catchers should have their own WAR, since only a catcher can replace a catcher). We can identify them by playing time, and we can futz around with the definition a little bit if we need to. Next, among those who aren't in that starting pool, we identify the top tranche of the 30 best bench players, which I would again identify by playing time, and then the second and third and fourth and so on. If a player were to disappear, his manager would probably want to take a guy from that top tranche of the bench to replace him. In a world where even the starters can slide around the field, that becomes more feasible.

We can take a look at that top tranche and say "How many of them showed that they are able to play (first, second, etc.)?" and therefore could have directly substituted for the starter? How many of them could have been a direct substitute for our injured player? We don't know whether one of them would be on *a specific* team, but we can say that 40 percent of the time, a manager would have been able to draw from tranche 1 in filling the role, and 35 percent from tranche 2. But on tranche 1, we can also look at how many of those players played a position that could have then shifted and covered for that spot. We'd need some eligibility criteria for all of this (probably a minimum number of games played) but it would just be a matter of multiplication. Shortstop would be harder to fill, and managers would probably be dipping a little further down in the talent pool, and so replacement level would be lower, as it is now.

Doing some quick analysis, I found that the difference in just batting linear weights (haven't even gotten into running or fielding) between tranche 1 and tranche 2 in 2019 was about 6.5 runs, prorated across 650 PA. Between tranche 1 and tranche 3, it's 10.8 runs. The ability to shift those plate appearances up the ladder has some real value.

This part is important. We can also give credit to starters for the positions that they showed an ability to play, even if they didn't play them (this is the guy fully capable of playing center, but who's in a corner because the team already has a good center fielder) because he allows a team to carry a player who hits like a left fielder to functionally be the team's backup center fielder. He facilitates that movement upward among the tranches. We can start to appreciate the difference between a left fielder who would never be able to hack it in center (and the compensatory move that his team would have to make) and the left fielder who could do it, but just didn't have to very often.

Past that, you can continue to use whatever hitting and fielding and running metrics you like to determine a player's value, but when we get down to constructing that baseline, I'd argue we need a better conceptual and mathematical framework. It's going to require some more #GoryMath than we're used to, but I'd argue it's a better conceptualization of the way that MLB actually plays the game in 2020. If…y'know…MLB plays in 2020. If WAR is going to be our flagship statistic among the *acronymati*, then we need to acknowledge that it contains some old and starting-to-be-out-of-date assumptions about the game. We may need to tinker with it. Here's my idea for how. ▪

—*Russell A. Carleton is an author of Baseball Prospectus.*

Secondhand Sport

by Patrick Dubuque

Back before time stopped, I liked to go to thrift stores. Now that I'm older, I rarely ever buy anything—I don't need much in my life, now—but I still enjoy the old familiar circuit: check to see if there are baseball cards to write about, look for board or card games to play with the kids, scan for random ironic jerseys, hit the book section. It takes ten, maybe fifteen minutes. Thrift stores are the antithesis of modern online shopping, because you don't know what they have, and you don't even really know what you want. It's junk, literal junk, stuff other people thought was worthless. That's what makes it great.

In an idealized economy, thrift stores shouldn't exist. Everybody has a living wage, and every product has a durability that exactly matches its desired life; nothing should need to be given away, no one should need to be given to. But then, thrift stores shouldn't work on a customer experience level, either. You wouldn't think an ethos of "let's make everything disorganized and hard to find" would lead to customer satisfaction, but low-budget retailers like TJ Maxx and Ross thrive on this model. People like bargain hunting as much for the hunting as the bargain; it's part of the experience, spending time as if it's a wager. There's a thrill, occasionally, in inefficiency.

In sports, the modern overuse of the word "inefficiency" is a condemnation: It insinuates that there is *an* efficiency, a correct way to be found, and that all other ways are wrong ways. It's prevalent in baseball but hardly contained to it; the lifehack, the Silicon Valley disruption are other examples of productivity creep in our daily lives. Their modern success makes plenty of sense. Maximization of resources, after all, is its own puzzle, and an industry of European board games is founded upon it. It's fun to take a system and optimize it, unravel it like a sudoku puzzle. If there's only one kind of genius, after all, there's no way anyone can fail to appreciate it.

Baseball has been hacking away at these perceived inefficiencies since its inception: platoons, bullpens, farm systems were all installed to extract more out of the tools at hand. But it's been a particular badge of the sabermetric movement, from Ken Phelps and his All-Star Team to Ricardo Rincon and the darlings of *Moneyball*. It's business, but it's also an ethos: the idea that there's treasure among the trash, something we all failed to appreciate until someone brought it to light.

It's the myth that made Sidd Finch so enticing, that fuels so many "best shape" narratives and new pitch promises. We all, athletes and unathletic sportswriters, want to believe that there's genius trapped inside us, and that it's just a matter of puzzling out the combination to unlock it. That our art, our style is the next inefficiency, waiting for our own Billy Beane. It's why we root for underdogs, and why we're excited for the Mike Tauchmans and the Eurubiel Durazos, champions of skin-deep mediocrity.

Except we aren't anymore, really. The days of "Free X" have descended beyond the ring of irony and into obscurity. There are still Xs to be freed, or at least one X, duplicated endlessly: Mike Ford, Luke Voit, Max Muncy. The undervalued one-dimensional slugger demonstrated how the game hasn't quite culturally caught up to its logical extreme. But for those who don't fit the rather spacious mold, times are grimmer. As Rob Arthur revealed several months ago, there's been a marked increase in the number of sub-replacement relievers. It's the outcome of a greater number of teams forced to play out games without the talent to win them, but it's also emblematic of the modern tendency of teams to dispose of their disposable assets, burning through cost-controlled arms the way that man chopped down forests in *The Lorax*. Stuff just isn't built to outlive their original owners anymore.

It's unsurprising, given how well-mined the market for inefficiencies has been of late. The disciples of the early analytics departments, and the disciples of those, have proliferated the league, with only a few backwater holdouts. The league has grown smarter, but every team has learned the same lesson. In fact, the phenomenon creates a peculiar kind of feedback loop: As teams value a specific subset of players or skills, prospective athletes learn to increase their own marketability by conforming themselves to the demands of their prospective employers.

And that's tragic, in the way that the extinction of animals is tragic; a certain amount of biodiversity in baseball has been lost. Shortstops hit like outfielders. Pitchers don't hit at all. Only the catchers remain idiosyncratic, thanks to the defensive demands of their position; eventually they too will be required to produce like everyone else, or they'll meet the fate of their battery mates. A perfect economy requires perfect production.

I mentioned earlier that more and more, I leave thrift stores empty-handed. It is true that I am more discerning than in the past; my bookshelves are full, and there are more streaming films than I will ever be able to watch. But there are other factors at play.

Thrift stores are, in a way, the bond markets of retail. When the economy is rough and other retailers are struggling, more people look secondhand for their products. But as recently as last year, publications were noting a reversal of the trend: Companies like Goodwill and Savers were expanding despite a strong economy. Publications credited a heightened sense of environmentalism and a rejection of cutting-edge fashion as drivers behind the increase, though the more likely answer is the modern American economy hasn't showered its favors equally, particularly among the young.

But it is more than just the economy. Baseball and thrift stores share something else in common, evident in our current conversations about restarting the sport: They live in the gray area between public service and private enterprise. Thrift stores provide affordable necessities to lower-class citizens, and collectibles and fashion for the middle-class. Because of the success of the latter, prices have gone up across the board. Especially in terms of clothing, the middle-class flight from fashion into vintage has instead carried the aftereffects of fashion, including its costs, into a territory where people just want clothes. But there's another factor in the rise of prices, in the form of the internet.

The Goodwills of the world have grown smarter, too, employing the internet to extract full value from their detritus. Ebay, similarly, has lost much of the charm it had as a new frontier around the turn of the century. Everything has a price point now; even individual taste is no match for the algorithm, because anything rare, no matter how niche its market, is a collectible to someone.

The internet has had the same effect on thrift stores that sabermetrics has had on baseball; its equivalent to OBP was the bar scanner. As detailed in Slate, the rise of second-party stores on eBay and Amazon birthed an entire industry of used-good salespeople, armed with PDAs and scanners, buying books for three dollars to sell online for five. The author, Michael Savitz, reports earning $60,000 by working nearly 80 hours a week; he makes it clear that this is not a vocation of his choosing. It's long hours, with no real creativity or individuality, skimming the cream off of a local establishment and flipping it to someone with a little more money on the other side of the country. And once the vocation exists, the obvious question arises: why wait to put the wares out on the shelves? Why allow value to exist at all?

Nothing is ruined. Thrift stores will continue to sell polo shirts and DVDs, and baseball will continue to exist and make or lose money, depending on who you believe. But as we continue to refine our knowledge, we lose something in the conquest for efficiency, a delight born out of the unknown. The problem isn't the efficiency itself; we can't blame the booksellers, or the people sweeping freeways to collect grams of platinum from damaged catalytic converters. The problem is a system that requires this sort of profit-skimming behavior in order to feed families (or, for corporations, maximize shareholder return).

In times like these, with the 2020 season on the brink and the collective bargaining agreement close behind, it can often feel like the current situation is untenable. It can't keep going like this, even if we don't know what to do about it. But as with thrift stores, there's an equally irresistible feeling that it *has* to keep going, that it would be unimaginable to not have this broken, amazing sport. Both industries exist on an invisible foundation of friction, of chaos and unpredictability, even as both see their foundations buffed down to a perfect, untouchable polish. But if COVID-19 and its financial ramifications do, as some have suggested, make it such that the baseball that returns is fundamentally different than the baseball that came before, perhaps this is the time to lean in, and change the game even more. Fix bunting. Make defense more difficult. Create viable, alternate strategies. Add some chaos back into baseball. It's fun when no one knows quite where things are. ■

—Patrick Dubuque is an author of Baseball Prospectus.

Steve Dalkowski Dreaming

by Steven Goldman

We dream of being a pitcher, of starring in the major leagues. Depending on your age and your sense of historical perspective, you might imagine yourself as Walter Johnson, throwing harder than anyone else—hitting more batters than anyone else, too, but always feeling bad about it. You could picture yourself as a Tom Seaver or a David Cone, with all the stuff in the world but still being cerebral about it, thinking about so much more than burning 'em in there. There are so many models one could choose: You could be a Lefty Gomez, Jim Bouton, or Bill Lee, skilled, but not taking the whole thing too seriously, or a Lefty Grove, Bob Gibson, or Steve Carlton, powerful but treating each start like a mission to be survived instead of a game to be enjoyed.

Very few would dream of being Steve Dalkowski, the former Baltimore Orioles prospect who died of COVID-19 last week at the age of 80. Yet, there is something just as noble in Dalkowski's negative accomplishments—and accomplishments is what they are—as there is in the precision-engineered pitching of a Greg Maddux. You have to be very good to be that bad. Dalkowski had all of the stuff of the greatest pitchers but none of the command; his story is not one of failing to conquer his limitations, but striving against one of the cruelest hands that fate or genetics or personality can deal us: A desire to achieve great things which is almost but not quite matched by the ability to meet that goal.

As with Johnson, Grove, Bob Feller, and the rest of the hard-throwing pitchers who played before the advent of modern radar guns, we have to take the word of the players and coaches who saw Dalkowski pitch as to his velocity. He was a hard-drinking, maximum-effort pitcher who, if their memories are to be believed, consistently threw over 100 miles per hour. His was the Maltese Fastball, the stuff that dreams are made of. The problem is that velocity without command and control is still a good distance from utility. Dalkowski was the most effective towel you could design for a fish, the sleekest bathing suit intended to be worn by an astronaut, but that doesn't mean he wasn't beautiful: We can appreciate a journey even if it doesn't end at the intended destination.

Whether because of sloppy mechanics he couldn't calm, an inability to understand that a consistent 98 in the strike zone would likely be more effective than a consistent 110 out of it, or all that beer, Dalkowski could never make the adjustments that pitchers like Feller and Nolan Ryan made before him, possibly because he had so far to go: Feller, who never pitched in the minors, came up at 17 and spent three years walking almost seven batters per nine innings before settling in at 3.8 beginning when he was 20. Ryan started out walking over six batters per nine but gradually improved as his long career played out; for him to go from 6.2 walks per nine with the 1966 Greenville Mets to 3.7 with the 1989 Texas Rangers represents a 40 percent reduction. An equivalent improvement by Dalkowski would still have left him walking over 11 batters per nine innings.

Dalkowski was like *The Room* of pitchers, a player so bad he became good again. Cal Ripken, Sr., who both played with and managed Dalkowski, recalled in a 1979 *Sporting News* "where are they now" piece the occasion when the pitcher crossed up his catcher and his fastball, "hit the plate umpire smack in the mask. The mask broke all to pieces and the umpire wound up in the hospital for three days with a concussion. If they ever had a radar gun in those days, I'll bet Dalkowski would have been timed at 110 miles an hour."

Signed by the Orioles out of New Britain High in Connecticut in 1957, Dalkowski was sent to Kingsport in the Appalachian League, where he pitched 62 innings. He allowed only 22 hits in 62 innings, or 3.2 per nine, a number with no equivalent in major league history (though Aroldis Chapman came close in 2014), and also struck out 121 (17.6 per nine) and walked 129 (18.7). He was also charged with 39 wild pitches. That June, one of his fastballs clipped a Dodgers prospect named Bob Beavers and carried away part of his ear. "The first pitch was over the backstop, the second pitch was called a strike, I didn't think it was," Beavers said last year. "The third pitch hit me and knocked me out, so I don't remember much after that. I couldn't get in the sun for a while, and I never did play baseball again." Former minor leaguer Ron Shelton based the *Bull Durham* pitcher Nuke LaLoosh on Dalkowski. And yet, to see him as a figure of fun, an amusing loser, is to misunderstand something unique and strange.

Dalkowski kept on posting some of the strangest lines in baseball history. Pitching for the Stockton Ports of the Class C California League in 1960, he struck out 262 and walked 262 in 170 innings. Yet, he did improve, especially after pitching for Earl Weaver at Elmira in 1962. Weaver had previously had Dalkowski at Aberdeen in 1959, but wasn't ready to grapple with him then. This time he was. "I had grown more and more concerned about players with great physical abilities who could not learn to correct certain basic deficiencies no matter how much you instructed or drilled them," he related in his autobiography, *It's What You Learn After You Know It All That Counts*. He got permission from the Orioles to give all of his players the Stanford-Binet IQ test. "Dalkowski finished in the 1 percentile in his ability to understand facts. Steve, it was said to say, had the ability to do everything but learn." [sic]

IQ tests are problematic diagnostic tools, so take Weaver's estimate of Dalkowski's mental capabilities with a grain of salt. What's important is that even if he got to the right answer by way of the wrong reason, Weaver had learned something valuable. His insight was to stop asking Dalkowski to learn new pitches and just let him get by with the two that he had. Were Dalkowski a prospect today, that would have been a no-brainer: Can't develop a third pitch? The bullpen is right over there, sir. Player development wasn't like that then, but Weaver, temporarily Dalkowski's mentor, could let him work with what he had. According to Weaver, the pitcher responded: "In the final 57 innings he pitched that season Dalkowski gave up 1 earned run, struck out 110 batters, and walked only 11." It's not true—as per the *Elmira Star-Gazette*, as of late July, Dalkowski had walked 71 in 106 innings and finished with 114 in 160 innings, which means Dalkowski's control actually faded at the end of the season rather than improved—but that doesn't mean it didn't happen in some sense, just that it didn't happen that way. Again, it's the journey, not the destination, and his ERA was 3.04 so *something* had gone right.

Also along the way: The next spring, Orioles manager Billy Hitchcock was rooting for Dalkowski to make the team as a long-man—maybe Weaver had gotten through to him. There were things out of Weaver's control, like the universe's twisted sense of humor: that March, Dalkowski's elbow went "twang."

You sometimes read that it was the Orioles' insistence on Dalkowski learning the curve that did him in, but even if they hadn't learned their lesson, the injury was probably just a coincidence: Dalkowski had thrown an incredible number of pitches over the previous few years. Still, it testifies to the dangers of trying to get what you want and risking the loss of what you had. Dalkowski tried to come back, but the 110-mph stuff was gone. A pitcher with no control and no stuff is...a civilian. What followed were years of vagabond living, arrests for drunkenness. There were Alcoholics Anonymous meetings, assistance from baseball alumni associations, but none of it took. From the 1990s until the time of his passing he dwelt in an assisted living facility, suffering from alcohol-related dementia. He'd been a heavy drinker since his teenage years. As with all those pitches per game, there was a price to be paid. You make choices on the journey and some of them are irrevocable. It's like a fairy tale: "Bite of poison apple? Don't mind if I do."

In the aforementioned *Sporting News* profile, Chuck Stevens, the head of the Association of Professional Ballplayers of America, a ballplayer charity, said, "I've got nothing against drinking. I do it myself sometimes. But, I don't condone common drunkenness. We went through lots of heartache and many dollars, but Dalkowski didn't want to help himself and we weren't going to keep him drunk." The journey is *un*like a fairy tale: No one will come along and kiss it better, not if they're busy forming judgments.

In the end, we are left with a sort of philosophical chicken/egg conundrum: Is failing to meet your goals evidence of unfulfilled potential or the lack of it? Isn't what you did by definition what you were capable of doing? Or could you have broken through to something better with the right help, the right lucky break? These are unanswerable questions, and how we try to answer them may say more about us than about the people we're judging.

No pitcher ever has it easy. *All* pitchers must work hard. *All* pitchers must refine their craft. It's almost never just about *stuff*. Dalkowski dreaming is no insult to the great pitchers who made it; from Pete Alexander to Max Scherzer, they have all earned their way up. And yet, if it is true that we can only do as much as we can do, then the journey would be more of an adventure, the ultimate triumph or defeat more noble, if like Dalkowski we lacked 100 percent of the confidence, the command, the self-possession, the commitment, the resistance to making bad decisions that so many great players possess—to be gloriously human. Or, to put it more succinctly, it would be fun to be able to throw as hard as any person ever has. Even if just for a moment, and even if nothing more came of it than that, no one could say you hadn't lived life to the fullest. ▪

—Steven Goldman is an author of Baseball Prospectus.

A Reward For A Functioning Society

by Cory Frontin and Craig Goldstein

O n July 5, Nationals reliever Sean Doolittle said in the middle of a press conference regarding the restart of Major League Baseball and what would later be known as summer camp, "sports are like the reward of a functioning society." This sentence was amidst a much longer, thoughtful reply about the societal and health conditions under which MLB players were being brought back. It's a very similar sentiment to one Jane McManus used on April 7, when she discussed the White House's meeting with sports commissioners. She said "sports are the effect of a functioning society—not the precursor."

Both versions of the same sentiment spoke to a laudable ideal in the context of a country that was not addressing a rampaging virus, and opting instead to bring sports back for the feeling of normalcy rather than the reality of it. "Priorities," as McManus said.

On Wednesday, the NBA's Milwaukee Bucks conducted a wildcat/political strike, refusing to come out for Game 5 of their playoff series against the Orlando Magic. The Magic refused to accept the forfeit, and shortly thereafter other playoff series were threatened by player strikes. Eventually the league moved to postpone that day's games, folding to players leveraging their united power.

The backdrop against which these actions took place was the shooting by police of Jacob Blake. Blake was shot in the back seven times by police, as he attempted to get into his vehicle. He managed to survive the assault, but is paralyzed from the waist down.

⚾   ⚾   ⚾

The step taken to walk out, first by the Milwaukee Bucks, then subsequently by other NBA, WNBA, and MLB teams, was a step toward upholding the virtue of the sentiment described by McManus and Doolittle. But that sentiment does not align with the broad history of sports in this and other countries, a history that contradicts the core of the idealistic statement.

Sports have been a significant part of American society for most of its existence, expanding in importance and influence in recent years. The idea that society was functioning in a way that was worthy of the reward of sports for most of that time is laughable. Much of America is not functioning and has not functioned for Black people, full stop. The oppressed people at the center of this political act by players, specifically Black players, in concert throughout the NBA and in fits and starts throughout Major League Baseball, have not known a society that functions for them rather than *because* of them.

Politics has been part of the sports landscape since the inception of sport, but for just about as long people have bemoaned its presence. Sports are to be an escape, it is said. An escape from what, though? A functioning society?

No, the presence of sports has never signified a cultural or political system that is on the up and up. Rather, the presence of sports *reflect and reinforce the society* that produces them.

⚾   ⚾   ⚾

The Negro Leagues were born out of societal dysfunction. The need for entirely separate leagues, composed of Black and Latino players barred from the Major Leagues because of racism? That is not a functioning society, and yet there were sports.

Even the integration of players from the Negro Leagues resulted in a transfer of power and wealth from Black-owned businesses and communities and into white ones, mirroring the dysfunction that had bled into every aspect of American society at the time. Japheth Knopp noted in the Spring 2016 Baseball Research Journal:

> *The manner in which integration in baseball—and in American businesses generally—occurred was not the only model which was possible. It was likely not even the best approach available, but rather served the needs of those in already privileged positions who were able to control not only the manner in which desegregation occurred, but the public perception of it as well in order to exploit the situation for financial gain. Indeed, the very word integration may not be the most applicable in this context because what actually transpired was not so much the fair and equitable combination of two subcultures into one equal and more homogenous group, but rather the reluctant allowance—under certain preconditions—for African Americans to be assimilated into white society.*

To understand the value of a movement, though, is not to understand how it is co-opted by ownership, but to know the people it brings together and what they demand. When Jackie Robinson—the player who demarcated the inevitability of the end of the Negro leagues—attended the March on Washington for Jobs and Freedom in 1963, he did so with his family and marched alongside the people. He stood alongside hundreds of thousands to fight for their common civil and labor rights. "The moral arc of the universe is long," many freedom fighters have echoed, "but it bends towards justice." The bend, it is less frequently said, happens when a great mass of people place the moral arc of the universe on their knee and apply force, as Jackie, his family, and thousands of others did that day.

⚾   ⚾   ⚾

Of course, taking the moral arc of the universe down from the mantle and bending it is not without risk. Perhaps the outsized influence of athletes is itself a mark of a dysfunctional society, but, nonetheless, hundreds of athletes woke up on Wednesday morning with the power to bring in millions of dollars in revenues. That very power, as we would come to find out, was matched with the equal and opposite power to *not* bring those revenues. That power, in hands ranging from the Milwaukee Bucks, to Kenny Smith in the *Inside the NBA* Studio, from the unexpected ally, Josh Hader, and his largely white teammates to the notably Black Seattle Mariners, would be exercised for a single demand: the end to state violence against Black people. Not unlike the March itself, it sat at the intersection of the civil rights of Black Americans and bold labor action. The March on Washington stood in the face of a false notion of integration—against an integration of extraction but not one of equality—and proposed something different. Just the same, the acts of solidarity of August 26, 2020 will be remembered in stark defiance of MLB's BLM-branded, but ultimately empty displays on opening weekend.

Bold defiance like this can never be without risk. By choosing to exercise this power, the Milwaukee Bucks took a risk. They risked vitriol and backlash from those they disagreed with. They risked fines or seeing their contracts voided, as a walkout like this is prohibited by their CBA. They risked forfeiting a playoff game, one that, as the No. 1 seed in the playoffs, they'd worked all year to attain. They didn't know how Orlando would respond. It wasn't clear that other teams throughout the league would follow suit in solidarity. And it wasn't known the league would accept these actions and moderately co-opt them by "postponing" games that would have featured no players.

If the league reschedules the games, some of the athletes' risk—their shared sacrifice—will be diminished, in retrospect. But they did not know any of that when they took that risk. And it is often left to athletes to take these risks when others in society won't, especially those of their same socioeconomic status and levels of influence.

It is athletes, specifically BIPOC athletes, that take them, though, because they live with the risk of being something other than white in this country every day. They are no strangers to the realities of police brutality. It seems incongruous then, to say that sports are a reward for a functioning society when we rely on athletes to lead us closer to being a functioning society. Luckily, our beloved athletes, WNBA players first and foremost among them, understand what sports truly are: a pipebender for the moral arc of the universe. ■

—Craig Goldstein is editor in chief of Baseball Prospectus. Cory Frontin is an author of Baseball Prospectus.

Index of Names

For the Joy of Keeping Score

THIRTY81 Project is an ongoing graphic design project focused on the ballparks of baseball. Since being established in 2013, scorecards have been a fundemantal part of the effort. Each two-page card is uniquely ballpark-centric — there are 30 variants — and designed with both beginning and veteran scorekeepers in mind. Evolving over the years with suggestions from fans, broadcasters, and official scorers, the sheets are freely available to everyone as printable letter-size PDFs at the project webshop: www.THIRTY81Project.com

Download, Print, Score, Repeat ...

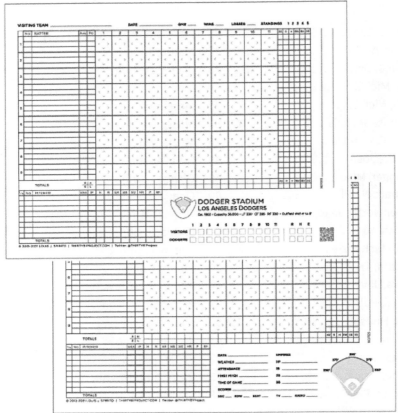